Hello!

Soft City was originally written in British English. The language has been modified from British spellings and terminology to their US equivalents. Therefore, words such as *lift*, *pavement*, and *lorry* now appear as *elevator*, *sidewalk*, and *truck*. One notable change is in the referencing of different floors of buildings. The British first floor is the second floor in US English.

Soft City

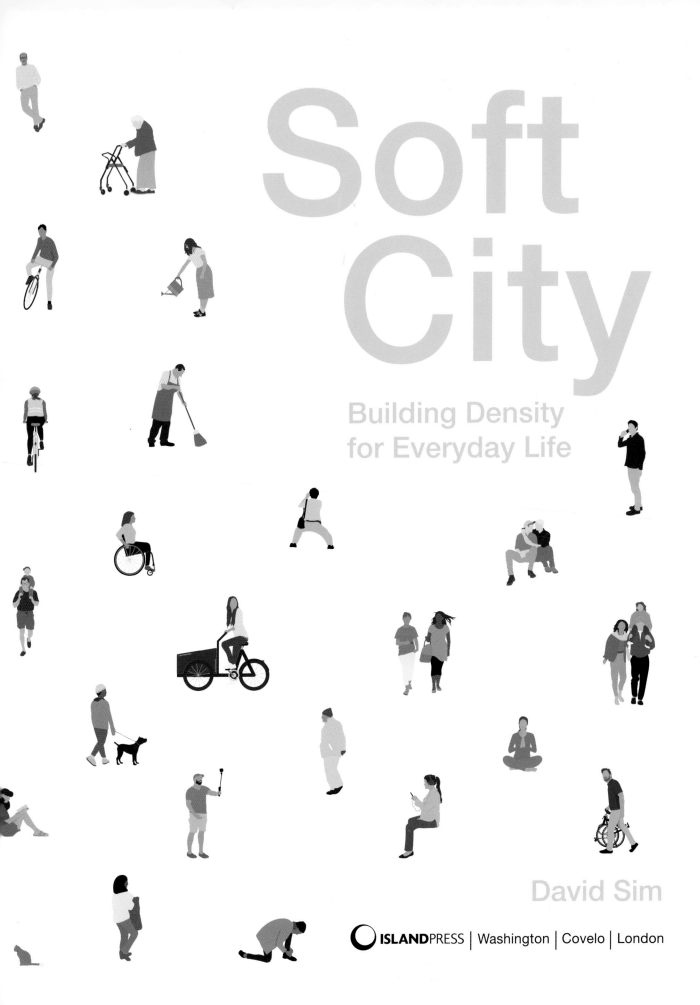

Soft City

Building Density
for Everyday Life

David Sim

ISLANDPRESS | Washington | Covelo | London

Library of Congress Control Number: 2018946755

All Island Press books are printed on environmentally responsible materials.

Project team
Birgitte Svarre, project manager
Marie Boye Thomsen, graphic layout
Scott Przibella, architect
Martin Nelson, project assistant
Camilla Siggard-Andersen, research assistant
Anne Louise Brath Severinsen, student assistant
Mads Kjær, student assistant
Elena Balabanska, student assistant
Anna Lindgaard Jensen, student assistant
Arianna Bavuso, student assistant
Samuel Csader, student assistant

Photographs in *Soft City* are mainly by the author. Special thanks to Lars Gemzøe for finding some harder-to-find motifs in his impressive collection.

This project was made possible with the financial support of Realdania, Denmark.

Manufactured in India by Imprint Press
10 9 8 7

Keywords: Climate change, communal space, community, Copenhagen, courtyard, cycling, enclosure, Dense-Low, density, human scale, hygge, mobility, nature, neighbors, spatial diversity, transit, walkability

What is the *soft* in soft city?

***Soft* is something to do with responsiveness**
accommodating, absorbing, supple, pliable, excusing, tolerant, flexible, elastic, extendable, adaptable, changeable, anti-fragile

***Soft* is something to do with ease**
simple, straight-forward, easy-going, effortless, smooth, intuitive, understandable

***Soft* is something to do with comfort**
comfortable, snug, safe, protected, sheltered, peaceful, quiet, "hyggelig"

***Soft* is something to do with sharing**
sociable, common, mutual, reciprocal, participatory, public

***Soft* is something to do with plurality**
joined-up, hybrid, mixed-use, overlapping, multifunctional, interconnected

***Soft* is something to do with simplicity**
low-tech, low-cost, low-key, modest

***Soft* is something to do with smallness**
human scale, human dimension, individual control, fractal, self-determining

***Soft* is something to do with appealing to the senses**
sensory, delightful, charming, seductive, intriguing

***Soft* is something to do with calm**
peaceful, quiet, cool, low-key, serene, tranquil, mild

***Soft* is something to do with trust**
sureness, clarity, certainty, confidence

***Soft* is something to do with consideration**
gentle, compassionate, sympathetic, empathetic, caring, benign, kindly

***Soft* is something to do with invitation**
welcoming, accessible, permeable, open

***Soft* is something to do with ecology**
a light touch, natural, seasonal, low carbon footprint

It's about ease, comfort, and care in everyday life.

Contents

Foreword by
Jan Gehl

In 1933, an exclusive group of European architects and city planners met in Athens to sign the radically game-changing CIAM Charter of City Planning. This charter, often referred to as the Athens Charter, dealt with future architecture and cities, and basically advised that various city functions from now on should be carefully separated: always keep residences, workplaces, recreation, and traffic apart. This approach was, not surprisingly, termed *functionalistic*, and the whole movement was referred to as Modernism. These ideas not only came to be the guiding principles for architecture and city planning for the decades that followed in the twentieth century, they became totally dominant worldwide. Especially after 1960, the Modernist planning principles came to be completely dominant, as rapid urbanization began to take place around the world. As part of this, the traditional focus on creating cities around spaces for people was changed to focusing on buildings surrounded by leftover spaces. Everywhere, Modernist ideas of freestanding, monofunctional buildings surrounded by vaguely defined no-man's-lands became the way to go. All in all, these new principles represented the most radical course change in the history of human settlement. And, by and large, there was never a proper assessment of whether these changes actually worked for mankind. They, in fact, did not work for mankind, as exemplified by the widespread discontent with these kinds of settlements.

In 1998, a new conference of European city planners was invited to Athens. Based on experience from the 65 years since the previous conference, a new Athens Charter was developed that basically says that residences, workplaces, recreation, and communications must never be separated. A complete turnaround!

Seemingly, it took 65 years and numerous Modernist city districts to reach this conclusion. However, a counter cities-for-people movement had been gradually developing for quite a number of years in reaction to the technocratic modernist movement.

In the area of writings and research, the work of Jane Jacobs in New York, and her famous 1961 book *The Death and Life of Great American*

Cities, stands out. Jane Jacobs raised the flag and excellently described many of the problems of Modernist city planning. She started to formulate new directions: look out of your windows; look at the people; look at life before you plan and design. In the years and decades following her call to arms, a number of researchers developed and deepened the work concerning how the built form influences quality of life. The New York School, with William H. Whyte, and later with the Project for Public Spaces, continues the work and inspiration from Jane Jacobs. In California, the Berkeley School, with Christopher Alexander, Donald Appleyard, Clare Cooper Marcus, Allan Jacobs, and Peter Bosselmann, contributed much valuable research and insights on people-oriented architecture and city planning over several decades.

In Copenhagen, a rather extensive research environment was established at the School of Architecture at the Royal Danish Academy of Fine Arts in the mid-1960s. For more than 40 years, this school continuously developed research in people-oriented architecture and city planning. I was a researcher at this Copenhagen School, along with Lars Gemzøe, Birgitte Svarre, and Camilla van Deurs, among others. The group produced a steady stream of books, with self-explanatory titles such as *Life between Buildings* (1971), *Public Spaces – Public Life* (1996), and *Cities for People* (2010). These and other "Copenhagen" books have, over the years, been spread to all corners of the world. The Copenhagen School has had a major influence on the development of Copenhagen into one of the world's most livable cities. This brand of people-oriented city planning has, over the years, been applied to many cities across the globe, such as Oslo, Stockholm, Sydney, Melbourne, London, New York, and Moscow.

Parallel to these various research efforts and their application in city-improvement projects, a number of significant people-oriented residential projects have been undertaken. Outstanding among these are the neighborhood and housing projects by the British-Swedish architect Ralph Erskine, created from the 1940s to his death in 2005. While the Modernists focused on freestanding, monofunctional buildings surrounded by far too much leftover space, Ralph Erskine focused on the people, the buildings, and the spaces between the buildings. This resulted in great neighborhoods, great site plans, and great architecture, with marvelous attention to the details, the people, and the city at eye level. Prominent projects from the office of Ralph Erskine include the neighborhoods of Sandvika, Tibro, Esperanza, and Ekerø in Sweden; Repulse Bay in Canada; and Byker Wall in Newcastle, England. Always much loved by the residents, Ralph Erskine came to have a significant influence on the art of making good neighborhoods, especially in Sweden. Professor Klas

Tham, who worked with Erskine for many years, designed the outstanding Bo01 neighborhood in Malmö, Sweden, discussed in this book. The development is very much in the spirit of Ralph Erskine. Other recent Swedish projects like Järla Sjö and Hammarby Sjöstad are also strongly influenced by the people-oriented "Erskine way of building."

In an interview in 2000, Ralph Erskine was asked what it takes to become a good architect. He responded, "To be a good architect, you have to love people because architecture is an applied art and deals with the framework of people's lives."

What does all this have to do with *Soft City* by David Sim? Actually, every word is relevant to understanding who David Sim is, his background, and where the idea of the soft city fits into the greater pattern of current trends in housing and city planning.

David Sim, another UK emigrant to Scandinavia, has—as a student, a teacher of architecture, and more recently as a partner and creative director at Gehl—been influenced significantly by the Copenhagen School. As an educator at the Lund School of Architecture, he has worked closely with a number of good "Erskinists," primarily Professor Klas Tham. David has had a very intensive people-oriented schooling. Good cities and good housing for people is indeed what concerns him, and what he addresses in this book. All the aforementioned influences and concerns are clearly seen in his careful descriptions of scenes from daily life and of the many details that must be addressed to create a truly soft city.

Soft City is a very personal book, reflecting David's outstanding interest in people and life. He draws from his great experience working on projects on all continents and in all cultures. You will benefit from his outstanding ability to see, to observe, and to reflect upon the scenes from life and cities. *Soft City* is an important addition to the growing literature on people-friendly architecture and city planning. Indeed, architecture and city planning need to be quite a bit more soft.

Here is a good place to start.

Jan Gehl
Copenhagen, April 2019

Preface

When I was 19 and an architecture student in Scotland, I first heard Jan Gehl's lectures. With a mixture of humility, humanity, and humor, Jan Gehl's common-sense approach weaves together architecture, planning, and psychology, with poignant observations of the human condition. From Jan I learned the huge significance of small, seemingly banal aspects of the everyday environment; the simple things, which influence our behavior and contribute to our well-being. I also learned that most of what I needed to know about how to design could be found by simply watching people and looking at the environment around me; by seeing what works and what doesn't.

These pragmatic ideals became the foundation for my future—for my continued education and professional practice. I studied in Denmark and Sweden, not only with Jan Gehl, but also with other architects who had become my personal heroes, including Steen Eiler Rasmussen, Sven Ingvar Andersson, Ralph Erskine, and Klas Tham. Living in Scandinavia, with its tradition of beautiful everyday architecture and design, I came to understand and appreciate an underlying respect for nature and humanity and a softer approach to daily life.

In 2002, I joined the fledgling Gehl Architects practice in Copenhagen. Since then, I have been working with an extremely dedicated, highly talented, and ever-growing group of people with the motto "making cities for people." At Gehl I have been given a platform to put my life's learnings into practice in projects around the world, as well as the opportunity to make this book. I would like to thank the Gehl team, especially my in-house editor Birgitte Svarre, who has supported me through this project over the last years, as well as my business partner, Gehl CEO Helle Søholt, who entrusted me with this task, and many others.

It would not have been possible to publish this book without the support of the Danish foundation Realdania that has a mission to create quality of life for all by developing the built environment. This book shares the mission of Realdania with its focus on the human dimension while considering the challenges of density, diversity, and livability. I hope this book will contribute to the making of better neighborhoods.

The process of writing this book has been long and sometimes painful, as I tried to decide what was worth sharing while also recognizing that there is so much I still don't know. Even with 25 years of professional practice, teaching, and research experience, I am still learning new things every day, and I continue to be a student of the human condition.

However, perhaps the wisest moment in my life as an urbanist came very early, at the age of five or six, with the living room floor strewn with Lego bricks. When my mother despaired, "When will this town of yours be finished?" I solemnly—and I think correctly—answered, "It's a town, mum. It'll never be finished."

David Sim
Copenhagen, 2019

Perhaps the wisest moment in my life as an urbanist came very early, at the age of five or six, with the living room floor strewn with Lego bricks. When my mother despaired, "When will this town of yours be finished?" I solemnly—and I think correctly—answered, "It's a town mum. It'll never be finished."

Introduction

From *Life Between Buildings* to *Soft City*

A Society can be so stone-hard
That it fuses into a block
A people can be so bone-hard
That life goes into shock

And the heart is all in the shadow
And the heart has almost stopped
Till some begin to build
A city as soft as a body

Inger Christensen, *It*, 1969[1]

There has been global interest in the Danish phenomenon of *hygge*, the everyday togetherness; the cozy, convivial atmosphere that promotes well-being. Hygge reflects the *softness* of Scandinavian societies. There is a gentle pragmatism, characteristic of the Nordic countries, where an exceptional quality of life for the many is built on a foundation of taking care of ordinary and everyday things, and making the best of limited resources (and arguably also reflected in the deeper values of the welfare state). This pragmatism is built on the possibilities and limits of human senses, by obeying laws of nature and living with the realities of climate and changing seasons.

The origins of *hygge* are the same as *hug* in English—literally to comfort. The Swedes call the same thing *mys* while the Norwegians have *kose* (like cozy). The Danish and Norwegian words can be turned into reflexive verbs, so you can you literally say "shall we cozy ourselves?" This telling linguistic detail in the cold climates and harsh landscapes of Scandinavia divulges a people's profound need to invest in mutual comfort, to *soften* the hard reality of daily life. Life still has its chores and challenges. Everyone still has to work, to go out into the winter cold, ride their bicycle or wait for their bus, pick up their children from daycare and make them dinner, do the dishes and put the rubbish out. But with a little care, they can do all of these things with a little more dignity, a little more comfort, and even with a little more pleasure. With small steps, and simple, low-cost investments, the hard reality of modern life can be somewhat *softened*—even in a world with rapid urbanization, increasing segregation, and climate challenges.

It may seem naïve to talk about *hygge* when facing some of the huge societal challenges of our time. A harsh political climate reflects a deep and heartfelt fear of change. There is fear of rapid urbanization, seen as potentially threatening people's way of life. There is fear of people, with increasing and changing populations, of overcrowding and congestion, social segregation, and inequality. There is a fear of climate change, unfamiliar weather patterns, and more frequent natural disasters. These challenges strike at the very core of the human condition. A common reaction when faced with fear is to run in the opposite direction, to deny the change and to shut out the differences rather than to embrace the challenges and welcome the opportunity of the new.

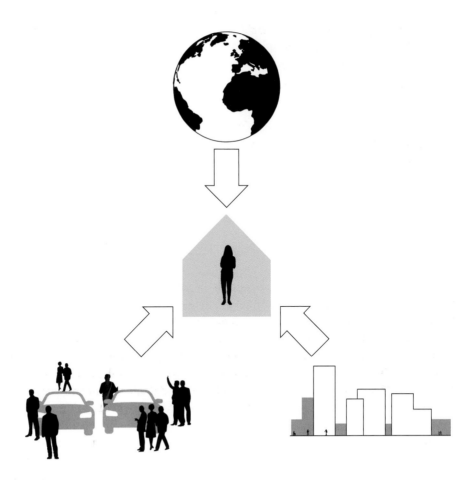

As cities densify around the world, and housing costs force more people into smaller spaces, balancing privacy and sociability becomes more difficult. Depression and loneliness have become normal phenomena. There is an epidemic of poor health due to people living their lives indoors, sitting inside mechanically ventilated buildings with artificial light, transporting themselves everywhere in cars. These are the challenges that *Soft City* addresses. Spending more time outdoors in the company of others, moving about, experiencing "life between buildings,"[2] is more important than ever.

Combining *soft* and *city* may sound as an oxymoron. It was in conversation with Professor Toshio Kitahara, the translator of Jan Gehl's books to Japanese, that the term *soft city* was identified. Professor Kitahara remarked on my frequent combination of these seemingly contradictory words. Soft city is about moving closer getting together, connecting people to one another and to all of the aspects of life around them. For decades, so much of urban planning has been focused on devising ways to reorganize human activity into distinct silos, to separate people and things and, by so doing, reduce the risk of conflict. I would like, instead, to focus on how potentially conflicting aspects of everyday existence can be brought together and connected to deliver better quality of life.

Perhaps soft city can be considered a counterpoint or even a complement to "smart" city. Rather than looking to complex new technologies to solve the challenges of increasing urbanization, we can instead look to simple, small-scale, low-tech, low-cost, human-centered, gentle solutions that help make urban life easier, more attractive, and more comfortable. Softer may be smarter.

This book presents observations about some basic aspects of urban form and urban design that can contribute to more sustainable and resilient communities and healthier and happier lives for the people who live in them. It is divided into three main chapters, each tackling one of the challenges of twenty-first-century life. A short essay appears between each chapter, each exploring a key idea about sustaining quality of life in urban environments.

The first chapter, "Building Blocks: Living Locally in an Urbanizing World," is about embracing the challenge of urbanization by finding ways to accommodate both density and diversity in the same place, making it possible to live as locally as possible. Chapter two, "Getting About and Getting On in a Congested World," is about both the physical and social challenge of people movement, starting right outside the front door. Chapter three, "Living with Weather in a Time of Climate Change," is about better connecting people living indoors to what is outside, to increase awareness of the forces of nature and make people more comfortable with them.

All of the chapters take small, simple steps from the more familiar (home and workplace) toward the less familiar (the wider neighborhood, city, and world). The chapters have a common thread of accommodating the density and diversity of everyday life in a way that delivers everyday comfort, convenience, conviviality, and community.

The book draws inspiration from a Nordic, human-centered planning tradition. In 1971, Jan Gehl published *Life Between Buildings*, in parallel to his wife, Ingrid Gehl, publishing *Bomiljø* (*The Psychology of Housing*).[3] These publications came at a watershed moment in planning, and represent a paradigm shift in the understanding of the human beings and their built environments. Jan and Ingrid Gehl created a cross-disciplinary approach to prioritizing human life over built form.

At the same time, a new form of urbanism was emerging in Denmark, the so-called Dense-Low, an architectural movement balancing the individual and the shared needs of residents. It was a "third way," combining industrial production techniques found in large-scale housing with typological details found in single-family homes.

The early Dense-Low projects radically reduced scale, making places with village-like patterns, with the individual homes distinctly recognizable. The homes were usually made distinct with small-but-significant details like their own front door and garden. Equal care was taken to create identifiable shared or common areas, designed to promote socializing between neighbors. Dense-Low celebrated both individuality and community. This important "both/and" of private *and* common recognized two seemingly contradictory sides of humanity: the need for individuality

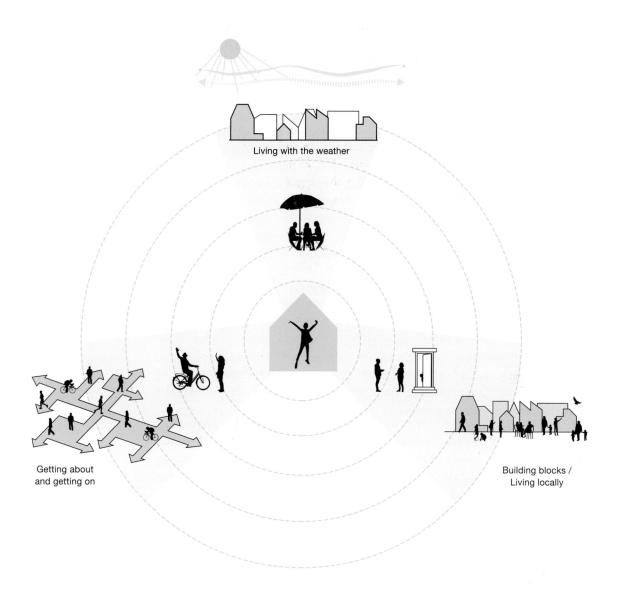

Living with the weather

Getting about
and getting on

Building blocks /
Living locally

Soft City embraces the opportunity to engage with planet, people, and place. At their own pace, people are invited to interact with their surroundings, moving from their homes and workspaces, step by step, outside, into their neighborhoods and into the wider world.

and the need for sociability. The principles in this book build on the values of the Dense-Low movement, updating them for the reality of the dense, mixed-use, urban environments of the twenty-first century.

At the same time as Dense-Low, streets and public spaces were beginning to be pedestrianized in Denmark, beginning with the famous *Strøget* in Copenhagen. For a while at least, these pedestrian streets offered a more sustainable and more convivial alternative to out-of-town, indoor shopping centers. As a response to the oil crisis of 1973-74, Danish towns and cities were also pioneering cycling as a serious form of transport. Urban cycling infrastructure made cycling safer for everyone while keeping the activity rooted in the urban context and very much a part of everyday life.

In the late 1970s and 1980s, Denmark saw a move away from the radical surgery of urban slum clearance in older areas, which had been promoted by Modernist planners across the world, to a more careful, thoughtful, local approach. The traditional structure of perimeter blocks was preserved, and many old buildings were preserved and renovated. The 1980s also saw ecological solutions being integrated into the urban contexts with solar panels and winter gardens bringing people closer to nature and making ecology relevant to their everyday lives.

When considered together, the Dense-Low housing, walking and cycling, simple changes and tweaks to the existing city blocks, and the integration of ecology, made urban living more sociable and considerably more attractive, especially to families with children. The recognition and care for the human dimension was instrumental in creating a renaissance in urban living and putting Copenhagen on the map as one of the most livable cities in the world.[4]

I don't have any ambition to Copenhaganize or Scandify the world. Rolling out solutions from one place into another requires considerable reinterpretation. However, the Nordic approach of embracing reality rather than trying to escape it might improve our lives. We can learn to celebrate the everyday rather than lament it, to live with the weather, live within our means, and live with the neighbors we have. This book includes examples from places outside of Scandinavia, including the rest of Europe, Japan, the US, and Australia, recognizing other resourceful places that seem to do more with less.

The urban world is made up of many different places with different climates and cultures, people and landscapes, politics and governance models, financing mechanisms and legal systems. Some of these differences are found among cities, towns, and villages, urban centers, and suburbs in the same country. Yet somehow around the world, despite all these differences, I see very similar situations, challenges, and problems. I suspect that the same basic principles can help deliver solutions for many of these situations. All in all, human beings and their behaviors are remarkably similar around the world, and so are their basic needs for comfort and conviviality in their everyday lives.

The current challenge of increasing urbanization is, in fact, an opportunity to make towns and cities work better. Cities have the potential to be places of beneficial interaction and platforms for connection, consciously juxtaposing the differences as they densify and diversify. We can create ever-evolving, gentle urban symbioses, discovering opportunities for healthier, more sustainable, more enjoyable and more meaningful relationships, by being neighbors.

As Jaime Lerner, architect and former mayor of Curitiba, Brazil, has famously said, "Cities are not the problem; they are the solution."[5]

**Some Principles
toward a Softer City**

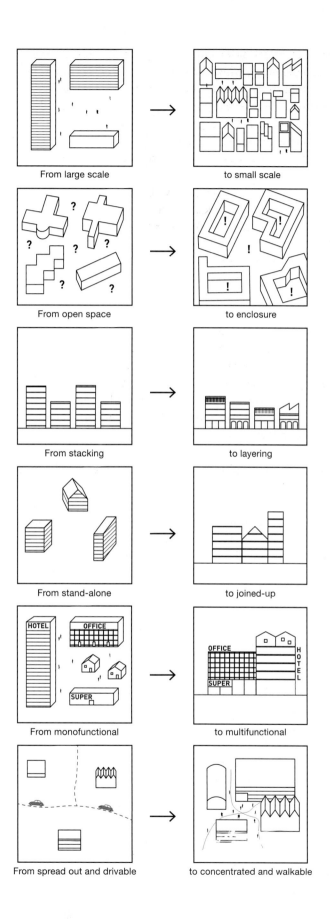

From large scale → to small scale

From open space → to enclosure

From stacking → to layering

From stand-alone → to joined-up

From monofunctional → to multifunctional

From spread out and drivable → to concentrated and walkable

Being Neighbors

01.

02.

03.

*"Neighborhood is not a place;
it's a state of mind"*

When talking about the human environment, towns and cities, urban design, or placemaking, the word *neighbor* is always useful. Think of your neighbor and you immediately think of another human being. It is not a vague planning concept or an unspecified urban phenomenon, but a living person, someone like you, but different. *Neighbor* is not a technical term or professional planning jargon, but a simple word that everyone knows and understands. At its simplest, *neighbor* can mean the person next door. At its broadest, it can mean all of humanity.

Neighborhood is a state of being in a relationship. More than anything, the human environment is about relationships: relationships between people and planet, relationships between people and place, and relationships between people and people.

In the relationship between people and the planet, we have made harsh places and severe climates habitable. Coexisting with other people has allowed us to cooperate and collaborate—to organize, trade, manufacture, and learn. Our ability to cultivate, control, and even manipulate these different relationships has allowed us to go beyond survival, to create societies and cultures, and often (but certainly not always) to achieve a better quality of life. Successful neighboring has allowed us to thrive and flourish, to live longer and fuller lives.

Of course, being a neighbor is not always easy. People have different perspectives and needs, values and behaviors. The benefits of colocation can just as easily become problems, as surplus becomes waste, energy becomes pollution, mobility become congestion, collaboration becomes exploitation, and coexistence becomes conflict.

Yet, in our rapidly urbanizing world, the word *neighbor* is more relevant than ever. All over the world, cities are not only densifying, but also diversifying. It is precisely the diversity and the differences that create opportunities. The simplest way to tap into everything society has to offer is to have neighbors, close neighbors.

Scenes of neighborhood:
01. Mexico City, Mexico
02. Copenhagen, Denmark
03. Stockholm, Sweden

The thesis of this book comes down to a simple equation:

Density x Diversity = Proximity

The idea is that the fusion of density and diversity increases the likelihood or the possibility of useful things, places, and people being closer to you.

The attraction of cities lies in mutual benefit. They offer reciprocal systems or arrangements, which support symbiotic relationships. There are at least three such benefits that can explain the attraction of a dense, diverse urban environment: physical proximity, common resources, and shared identities.

Physical proximity to people and places can improve access to employers and employees, teachers and tradesmen, shops, schools, and services where and when you need them. Proximity in an urban context is made possible by common resources such as public spaces, hospitals, libraries, universities, and public transport. It is about being closer to where decisions and discoveries are made, where new knowledge grows, where fashion is created, trends start, and culture happens.

With proximity, the space of the urban environment can be translated into time, with the convenience of being able to do a wide variety of things in the same day, in the same morning, or even in the same hour.

We know that infrastructure costs per capita decrease as density increases. Additionally more people make for more customers, allowing a wider range of commercial and cultural activities to thrive. In theory, the larger the city, the larger the pool of common resources. It is exactly this access to these that compensates for the sometimes cramped and crowded living conditions of urban life.

Another benefit is having a shared identity with your community, which comes from sharing the same places and resources. This feeling of belonging can be seen in people's pride in their city, in its places and local heroes, its public buildings, parks, and promenades, and its athletes and artists. Local urban identity is often stronger and perhaps more relevant than national, cultural, or ethnic identity. Its inclusive nature arguably makes for one of the healthiest forms of collective identity.

Yet another benefit of dense, diverse urban environments is the potential for unexpected opportunities. Towns and cities are sites of the spontaneous and serendipitous random encounters and unpredictable meetings. The ever-changing configuration of people results in a delightful unpredictability, rife with possibilities. Seemingly an insignificant aspect of urban life, it has very real importance.

If we better understand what conditions make for being good neighbors, we can then better accommodate density, difference, and change. We can embrace these as beneficial opportunities rather than unfortunate challenges.

We should recognize that every detail in the physical composition of the built environment has the potential to deliver comfort, convenience, and connection to others. The subtle balance of private and public needs, and the colocation of different activities in the same place make it possible to live well without having to travel so much. By getting the relationships right in the physical environment, with everything you need close at hand, an urban neighborhood can offer a better life.

With everyday exposure and regular encounters comes relevance. With time, this awareness and understanding can grow into reverence, when people care about planet, people, and place. Changing mindsets leads ultimately to changing behaviors.

In this way, neighborhood is not a place; it's a state of mind.

Kissa Laundry Café, Tokyo, Japan. An empty ground floor in a quiet neighborhood was creatively converted into a café and laundry that quickly became a popular community hub.

Building Blocks

Living Locally in an Urbanizing World

Public Front

Joined-up buildings

Layered building

Penthouse

Common s

Active ground floor

Together

Velo

16

There are many arguments for increasing density. With rapid urbanization and dwindling resources, we have to use existing infrastructure more efficiently, make better use of the resources we have—specifically the space we have—and make what we build work harder for us. Greater density alone is not going to give us better lives. No real benefit comes from being stacked on top of one another just because it is more spatially efficient.

True urban quality comes from accommodating density and diversity of building types and uses in the same place. I believe that different, even conflicting, uses and users can coexist and enjoy the convenience of colocation if they are accommodated in an urban framework that lets them be good neighbors to each other.

Making the most of the roof

Private back

Enclosure

Courtyard

Enclosure

The urban pattern of enclosure seems to be as old as the built environment itself. Ever since the very first formal human settlements, thousands of years ago, there has been a simple pattern of building that could be called *urban*. The urban pattern is characterized by building to the very edge of the property rather than in the middle, and having joined-up buildings, where different properties are juxtaposed. Perhaps the most significant aspect of this urban pattern is the different outdoor spaces created between the buildings. By grouping buildings to make enclosures, extra, *controllable* outdoor spaces are created at no extra cost.

The enclosures between the buildings or inside the block give privacy and security, which are much-needed qualities in an urban environment. The fact that the space is protected, physically and visually, means it lends itself to useful activities, either as an extension of life inside the buildings or as an additional, complementary space where other activities can happen. Protected spaces make room for flexibility over time, for temporary or seasonal uses, and for future expansion. They also contain noise, smell, and mess, thus sparing the surrounding neighbors from potentially annoying activities. In this way, these protected outdoor spaces can be seen as zones of tolerance and have a vital role in buffering humans and their activities from each other.

When multiplied, groups of blocks create other types of spaces: streets and other public spaces like squares that also come at no extra cost. These spaces are important, even though they are usually not completely enclosed. They are defined by the edges of the blocks, allowing access between them. A level of containment ensures they are weather-protected places, making movement through them and time spent in them more comfortable. This ancient urban pattern of building has the advantage of creating two very different kinds of useful outdoor spaces—one private and the other public. The spatial economy of the system allows these different kinds of space—built and unbuilt, private and public—to coexist in close proximity to each other, separated only by the buildings themselves. Using the minimum material and space to enable different activities to develop, this pattern solves the greatest challenge in urban design, which is accommodating density with a diversity of building types and uses.

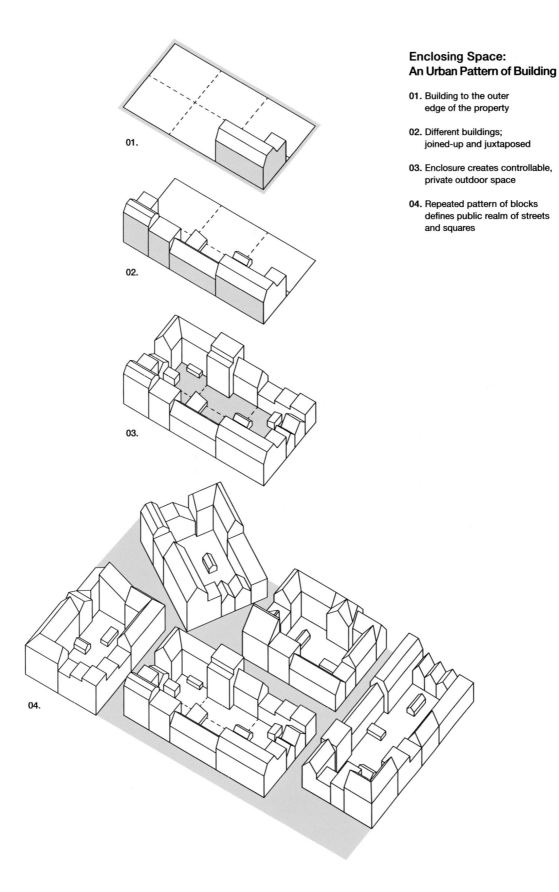

Enclosing Space: An Urban Pattern of Building

01. Building to the outer edge of the property

02. Different buildings; joined-up and juxtaposed

03. Enclosure creates controllable, private outdoor space

04. Repeated pattern of blocks defines public realm of streets and squares

01.

02.

03.

04.

There are many variations on the enclosed form, ranging from one big courtyard enclosed by a single building where the entire block is effectively one property, to multiple buildings surrounding a number of subdivided outside spaces. From the hutong to the patio, the Hof and the cloister, there are examples of enclosed urban blocks in different climates and cultures, throughout the history of urban settlement. The outdoor space enclosed by buildings is a universally useful and relevant habitation form in urban contexts. What is key is that the inner space is clearly defined and recognizable, and controllable by the occupants of the surrounding building or buildings.

A key characteristic of the urban pattern of enclosure is its ability to deliver density with lower heights. By building all around the outer edge of the plot, creating what might be called a *crust* of buildings around the void inside, a larger footprint for buildings is possible. This very efficient way of utilizing space allows the largest surface for building on, meaning the height of the buildings can be lower. Smaller blocks have more edge, or crust, created by the buildings, relative to their size than larger blocks. Therefore, the same number of square meters of building can be delivered at lower heights if the blocks are smaller.

A classic urban block with around four or five stories does much more than its modest appearance might suggest. When developed to its full potential, the enclosed block can create a symbiotic urban system for many different, co-located activities. The combination of density and diversity of building types and uses, with a compact footprint and on a human scale, makes for an environment that is both efficient and attractive. With its front and back, the enclosed block gives both a clearly defined, open, and accessible public side, as well as a protected and controlled private side. This simple approach accommodates a wide variety of needs, from very public to very private, in close proximity.

The spatial organization of the enclosed block helps to accommodate the diverse demands of everyday life with more options for where different kinds of activities can take place. The front is public, with the ground floor providing an ideal place

Dragør, Denmark and Rosengård, Malmö, Sweden. The picturesque Danish village of Dragør (left) is famous for its microclimate, which allows fig trees to grow in its small gardens despite the relatively cold and windy northern climate. It's hard to comprehend that the village made up of cottages and laneways has the same density as the Rosengård housing estate in Malmö (right) with its large slab blocks.

Different Built Forms Delivering the Same Density

The same built density can be delivered with very different building typologies and very different in-between spaces. The four examples of built form shown here have the same density. Each has a total floor area of 22,400 m² (241,000 sq. ft). What is important is the usefulness of the different built forms. The notable aspects are the proportion of enclosed or protected outdoor space that can be more useful than undefined open space, the proportion of building edge that can help create useful street frontage, and the proportion of the ground floor and the top floor (or penthouse), as these can be more useful and attractive, and often have greater economic value.

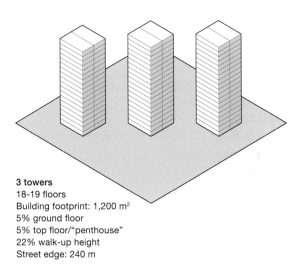

3 towers
18-19 floors
Building footprint: 1,200 m²
5% ground floor
5% top floor/"penthouse"
22% walk-up height
Street edge: 240 m

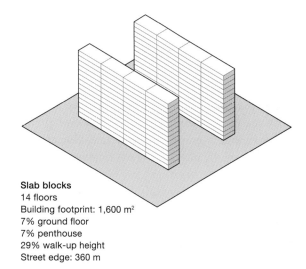

Slab blocks
14 floors
Building footprint: 1,600 m²
7% ground floor
7% penthouse
29% walk-up height
Street edge: 360 m

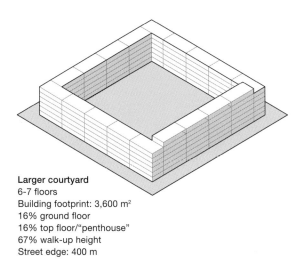

Larger courtyard
6-7 floors
Building footprint: 3,600 m²
16% ground floor
16% top floor/"penthouse"
67% walk-up height
Street edge: 400 m

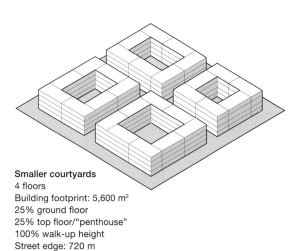

Smaller courtyards
4 floors
Building footprint: 5,600 m²
25% ground floor
25% top floor/"penthouse"
100% walk-up height
Street edge: 720 m

for service functions, shops, and businesses. The back is private and provides a safe place for children to play or a sensible place to store property.

The walls of buildings help to ensure that the noise from streets and public spaces, especially of traffic, is kept out. There is a great value to peace and quiet in the dense city, and the enclosure can even make it possible to sleep with an open window toward the courtyard. The built enclosure can also block air pollutants, which means cleaner air for ventilation, and washing can be hung out to dry.

Although the urban pattern of the enclosed block predates the existence of motorized vehicles, it is practical for dealing with them. Vehicle access to buildings is necessary for emergency services, deliveries, and picking up or dropping off at the door. However, motorized vehicles bring with them noise, fumes, and the potential for accidents. The solution is to keep the vehicles outside of the enclosure, creating a vehicle-free space on the inside. The enclosed block can deliver the best of both worlds, as there is easy access right up to the front door of the building and a safe, clean, and quiet outdoor space just at the back door.

This pattern of enclosure is not without its failings. You will not have to look hard to find places where the system of enclosed blocks and courtyards is compromised, with the open spaces eaten up by greedy buildings, destroying the usefulness, comfort, and tolerance of the system. Sometimes, the courtyard is reduced to a dirty storage facility, or a place for outdoor toilets and bins. However, in many other places, the courtyard has been rediscovered and turned into a vital shared resource that is light, green, and airy.[6]

The enclosed block can also make its own weather. The perimeter of the block shelters the inner space from the wind, while the variation in the dimensions of the courtyard space or spaces and in the height or heights of the surrounding buildings can let in more or less direct sunshine. The courtyard can be a wind-protected suntrap or a shady oasis, depending on what is appropriate in the context of the local climate. The enclosure can offer greater control as well as greater consistency of microclimate and this can allow residents to spend more time and do more things outside.

01. **Lund, Sweden.** A shared, sheltered courtyard garden provides useful outdoor space for family events in the middle of the city.

02. **Malmö, Sweden.** As well as creating a comfortable microclimate, the courtyard is a common social focus for the residents.

03. **Freiburg, Germany.** For resident children, the large common courtyard makes a play area far larger than a private garden.

04. **Mexico City, Mexico.** The patio is a common built form in Latin countries. Here, as part of a museum, it functions as a more formal outdoor exhibition space.

05. **Hackesche Höfe, Berlin, Germany.** The dense system of courtyards accommodates a wide range of uses and users in a highly flexible, integrated, and accessible system.

06. **Breitenrain, Berne, Switzerland.** A covered passage from the street leads to a lush and quiet inner courtyard.

07. **8 House, Copenhagen, Denmark.** A new interpretation of the common courtyard.

01.

02.

03.

04.

05.

06.

07.

01.

02.

03.

04.

05.

06.

01. **Copenhagen, Denmark.** The common focus of a shared space between a large but limited group of neighbors, a place to encounter and engage with others on a controlled, neutral territory.

03. **Copenhagen.** A protected microclimate between the buildings where greenery can flourish as well as a space for common furniture and play equipment.

05. **Copenhagen.** An accessible, secure place with cleaner air to hang laundry to dry.

02. **Copenhagen.** A large and easily accesible shared back garden with many potential playmates—safe from traffic and with plenty of surveillance.

04. **Copenhagen.** A secure place to leave out toys (and other personal property) overnight

06. **Tübingen, Germany.** A common focus for different people (different buildings and tenures) thanks to the shared courtyard.

The Potential of Smaller Blocks:
Donnybrook Quarter, London, England

Photo: Morley von Sternberg

The Donnybrook Quarter social housing project is an example of low-rise, high-density housing that is also low-cost and high-quality. Two new streets were introduced, creating smaller blocks within the site. In addition to creating new public space where one street widens to become a square and improving walkability with new local shortcuts, these smaller blocks create more street edge and allow the required density to be delivered with buildings of just two and three stories. The lower heights accommodate individual houses, each with their own front door and walled courtyard garden, using a simple and affordable form of construction.

Here at Donnybrook Quarter, the foundation of small-scale blocks and individual components, make for an intensive-yet-sensitive solution to urban living, proving that human scale and intimacy are possible at higher densities.

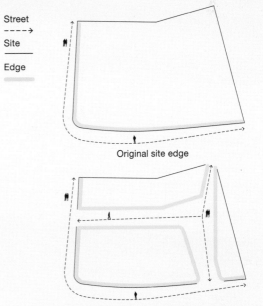

Street

Site

Edge

Original site edge

Site edge increased by sub-dividing into smaller blocks.

The Courtyard that Does More:
Dronningensgade, Copenhagen, Denmark

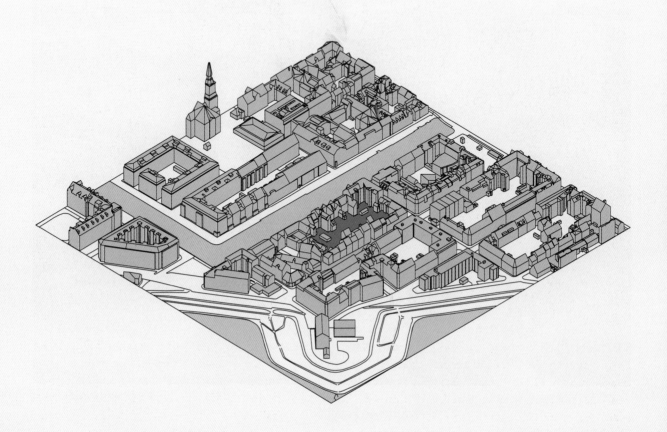

Build Density

Total area: 400 x 400 m, 1,300 x 1,300 feet
Total floor area: 235,600 m²/2,536,000 sq. ft
Housing floor area (gross):   150,100 m²/1,615,600 sq. ft
Office floor area (gross):   85,500 m²/92,500 sq. ft
Gross floor area ratio: 1.47
Site coverage ratio: 0.29

People Density

Number of residents: 2,998
Number of units: 1,898
Number of residents per unit: 1.57

Mix of Functions

This part of the neighborhood of
Christianshavn has a mix of functions:

- housing with different ownerships
- student housing
- restaurants and cafés
- community facilities
- supermarket
- small shops
- offices and institutions

The eighteenth-century, traditional blocks along Dronningensgade Street in Copenhagen's Christianshavn district are a model example of what the enclosed-block form can accomplish. Within what is a fairly dense block is a remarkable diversity of spaces and buildings. The area shows how very simple differentiations in the spatial organization can allow far more to happen, not just for the diversity of buildings, but also for the diversity of its open space.

In the northernmost block, located next to a public square and close to the main thoroughfare, various non-residential uses have flourished alongside a range of dwelling types, including a student residence. The active ground floors include small shops, offices, and services, a "bodega" pub, a cellar restaurant and music venue, and a nursery school with big front windows. There is a co-op supermarket that has progressively expanded into neighboring buildings, including a former cinema and a bank, creating an important local shopping hub. The courtyard includes a nursery for the smallest children and a shared laundry for the student housing.

The block has organically evolved into a robust urban form. The many changes over time can be seen in the architectural styles, which are extremely varied, ranging from the traditional vernacular, classical, 1930s functionalist, and 1970s social modern. The neighboring block to the south (indicated in green on the diagram on p.26) is perhaps even more interesting, as the spaces between the buildings have been partially redeveloped in an urban renewal program to create higher-quality outdoor spaces.

The variation in styles, ages, and types of buildings gives the streets plenty of character. There are larger apartment buildings alongside small townhouses, older construction and newer infill. Each building has its own particularities, which helps to give the streets a distinct neighborhood identity.

Connected Outdoor Greenspace

The traditional Copenhagen block is made up of multiple buildings fronting the street, each with its own back courtyard. Historically, the courtyards

01.

03.

02.

were hard surfaces with smaller outbuildings—toilets, wash houses, storerooms, workshops—rather than green spaces and gardens. As part of an urban renewal project on this particular block, the courtyards have cleared of walls and most outbuildings, while new soft landscaping has been added. It is an early example of the courtyard greening program that the City of Copenhagen established to improve inner-city living. This program is key in upgrading the existing building stock in Copenhagen.

As with other urban blocks, the fronts and backs of the buildings create two different worlds: there is public life on the outside, facing toward the street, and private life on the inside, in the courtyard. Each building addresses the street with windows and its own front door or entrance passage. This means that there is a feeling that life indoors is somehow connected to the street, and that comings and goings are frequent.

Courtyard Entrances

There are multiple entrances to the block's inner world, with private back doors or shared staircase entrances as well as gated passageways between buildings. Usu-

ally the common courtyard is not locked and can be accessed by the public. However, the very clear spatial order reflects a sense of social control, which should be respected by any guests.

Distinct Layers of Outdoor Space

The urban renewal program added small, completely private spaces to the inner courtyard for the ground-floor apartments. There are two other distinct layers of outdoor space in the inner courtyard. One comprises the old, individual courtyards closest to the buildings, which are partly preserved but now somewhat greener. The other includes the large, communal green space in the middle. Each of these layers of outdoor space invites different kinds of activities and behaviors.

The communal green space is large enough to accommodate group activities such as social gatherings and games, as well as shared equipment (like a barbeque and sandbox) and furniture. This space gives the residents in the block a place to congregate on what is perceived as neutral or common ground. Because this is a private, shared space, it represents the common interests of the neighbors who share ownership.

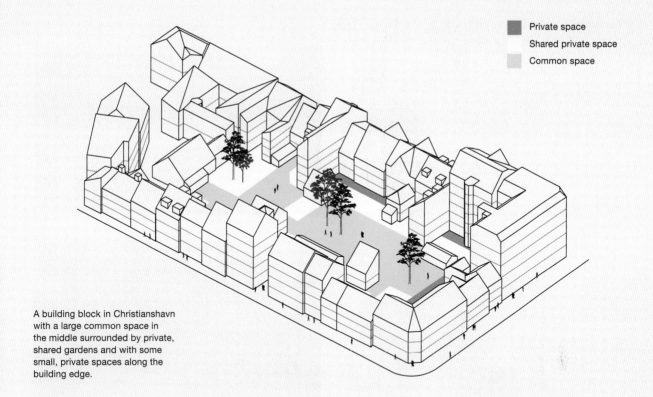

A building block in Christianshavn with a large common space in the middle surrounded by private, shared gardens and with some small, private spaces along the building edge.

People with front doors on different streets, who may not have realized that they were neighbors, have the opportunity to meet in this inner space. A small but thoughtful detail is the common toilet. This is very useful for group events or for children playing outside, saving a trip inside. The cleanliness of the toilet reflects the level of common responsibility.

While the older, individual courtyards are also communal spaces, they are shared by a smaller group of residents. They tend to have a stronger sense of identity than the communal green space in the middle. These shared yards are places where toys, bicycles, or prams might be left out. In these spaces, outdoor projects might be tolerated, with residents leaving out their materials and tools overnight. There might be shared outdoor furniture where residents can entertain their own guests.

The completely private gardens, decks, or balconies help to buffer the ground-floor residents from the activity of the courtyard. These are useful spaces, directly connected to the rooms inside where residents can relax, hang laundry, and store possessions. These outdoor spaces make the ground-floor apartments

more attractive. The raised deck or balcony adds to the feeling of privacy.

As well as the three distinct kinds of outside space, the positioning of the outbuildings (old and new), including cycle sheds and storage bins, add to the spatial complexity of the courtyard. In addition to their practical uses, they visually divide the courtyard into smaller spaces, creating extra inhabitable edges and bringing a degree of intimacy to the spaces. They ensure that we can't see everything at once, making for a continual sense of discovery.

Particularly for younger children, this complex courtyard space offers a spectrum of play opportunities with a range of different territories, suitable for different kinds of play at different ages, all accessible without having to go beyond the boundaries of home or to cross a trafficked street.

01. Different properties, each with their own small back garden.

02. Common play space in the middle of the block.

03. Shared backyard.

A Range of Spatial Experiences All In the Same Place

01.

01.

02.

02.

03.

03.

04.

04.

01. Private, outdoor spaces directly connected to indoor living space.
02. Shared courtyard for one building accessible from both the building and the common space in the middle of the block.

03. Large, common space in the middle of the block accessible for all.
04. The fronts of the buildings connect directly to the public realm of the street.

The Green Courtyard Program, City of Copenhagen, Denmark

When many of the courtyards in Copenhagen were built in the nineteenth century, they were filled with outbuildings, including outside toilets, small industrial workshops, and storage facilities. Most ground surfaces were paved, and there was little or no vegetation. In 1992, the City of Copenhagen established a program called Green Courtyards, with the goal of giving the inhabitants green space for relaxing right outside their backdoor.

The inhabitants in the buildings surrounding the communal courtyard, regardless of tenure, are required to establish an association to obtain city funds for the renovation of the courtyard. After renovation, the association is responsible for the maintenance of the courtyard. The renovation of the courtyards has resulted in more use and interaction. This citywide initiative has been crucial in encouraging families with children to live in the city. More recently, stormwater management elements have been integrated into the program.

01.

01. **Hedebygade, Copenhagen.** Renovated courtyard with different kinds of greening.

02./03. **Nøjsomhedsvej, Copenhagen.** Before and after the renovation of a courtyard. The redesign demonstrates how the removal of fences between properties, direct access from ground floor, better organization of recycling bins, as well as a greener and more appealing design all make a big difference despite the narrow shape of the courtyard. Photos: City of Copenhagen.

02.

03.

Enclosure with Multiple Uses:
"Jim's House," Västergatan, Malmö, Sweden

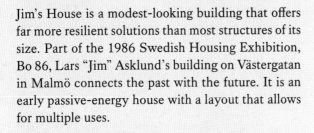

01. Photo: Lars Asklund

02. Photo: Lars Asklund

Jim's House is a modest-looking building that offers far more resilient solutions than most structures of its size. Part of the 1986 Swedish Housing Exhibition, Bo 86, Lars "Jim" Asklund's building on Västergatan in Malmö connects the past with the future. It is an early passive-energy house with a layout that allows for multiple uses.

Many of the common-sense architectural solutions found in Jim's House echo traditional design: the generous entrance passage; the L-shape plan of the main building, with a wing extending into the back; the L-shaped, inward-facing courtyard building; and the inward-sloping roofs that let sunlight into the sheltered outdoor spaces. It has two courtyards—an outer, hard-paved one closer to the street, and a private inner courtyard with soft landscaping. Jim's House has shopfronts on the ground floor. The extra wing

allows the accommodation of apartments of different sizes, making for an implicit social and economic mix. The apartments function equally well as workspaces.

Asklund made the outside space work just as hard as the building, buffering each concentrated use from the next while providing much-needed extra living space in a dense, urban context. The two L-shaped buildings define the outdoor spaces with their inhabited edges, making significant places rather than leftover space. The courtyard pavilion in the middle separates the hard and soft courtyards.

The private, inner courtyard is protected from the elements, creating extra living space. The north-facing street facade has smaller windows with pronounced mullions, which make for better insulation and helps to create some privacy.

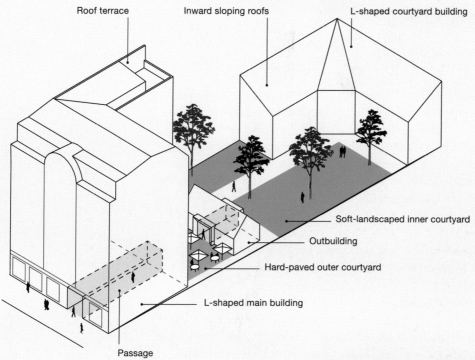

Roof terrace

Inward sloping roofs

L-shaped courtyard building

Soft-landscaped inner courtyard

Outbuilding

Hard-paved outer courtyard

L-shaped main building

Passage

01. The north-facing street facade with small windows and shop fronts.
02. The inner courtyard looking back at the main building.
03. A temporary restaurant in the outer courtyard.

This double-courtyard system created two distinct outside spaces, which invite different uses and thus a degree of flexibility. For example, the front, paved courtyard has functioned as a delightful summer over-spill for the ground-floor restaurant. Restaurant guests are permitted to enter the private area and dine in the sun, enjoying the clean air and the peace and quiet. Even if only for a few hours a day, the north-facing restaurant can flourish in the summer months. The central pavilion acts as a buffer for the other part of the courtyard. The diners can view the inner court-yard, but the design makes it clear that it is private. The double-courtyard system is eminently practical, with a hard surface for service functions—bins, bikes, occasional restaurant tables—and a more lush and tranquil inner world of the courtyard garden for the pleasure of the residents. At the time of completion, critics were unable to see past the postmodern street facade. Jim's House is a model for a flexible, livable, environmentally sustainable, mixed-use building. It is a clear case of the difference between what a build-ing superficially looks like and what it actually does.

03.

Joined-up

Different plots on the same block can be developed and managed independently. This makes for greater flexibility in building design, typology, construction method, delivery, tenure, use, and, crucially, development over time. Subdivision of the land allows for construction by multiple developers and designs by many different architects. The plot and building dimensions can vary. However, each plot must have one edge adjacent to the street for access. There is a need for some common sense in the geometry as the less rectangular the plots are, the less efficient they are to build on.

Each plot can exist independently from its neighbors, but they must have a firewall and independent access to ensure the integrity of the block as a whole.

To connect the buildings to one another, they must have a firewall: a blank, windowless wall on either side. This basic structure allows for the juxtaposition of buildings. It also saves a considerable amount of space that is wasted when there are gaps between the buildings. Any extensions or wings of the street building or any outbuildings should also have a firewall where they touch the edge of their plot. These firewalls allow the neighboring plots to develop independently.

The double wall created by the side-by-side construction helps to insulate the buildings, reducing noise and vibration. Additionally, use of a firewall reduces construction and maintenance costs because there is less exposed wall surface than with freestanding buildings.

Every plot should have at least one independent access point from the street, connecting through the building to the inner courtyard space. This means every plot, and its building or buildings, can function independently of the other plots on the block.

Of course, there are exceptions. In old, urban quarters there are unplanned gaps between buildings, with eccentric windows on sidewalls, and improvised access arrangements. However, in general terms, firewalls and independent access ensure the independence of each building plot over time. The independence of each element in an enclosed block is not just a question of physical form or design. In the long life of a building after its construction, the individual people or organizations that own or manage it can develop their own approaches to running, maintaining, and commercializing their property. Some buildings might be strictly controlled for single use, others extremely mixed. Some may allow subletting and others may not.

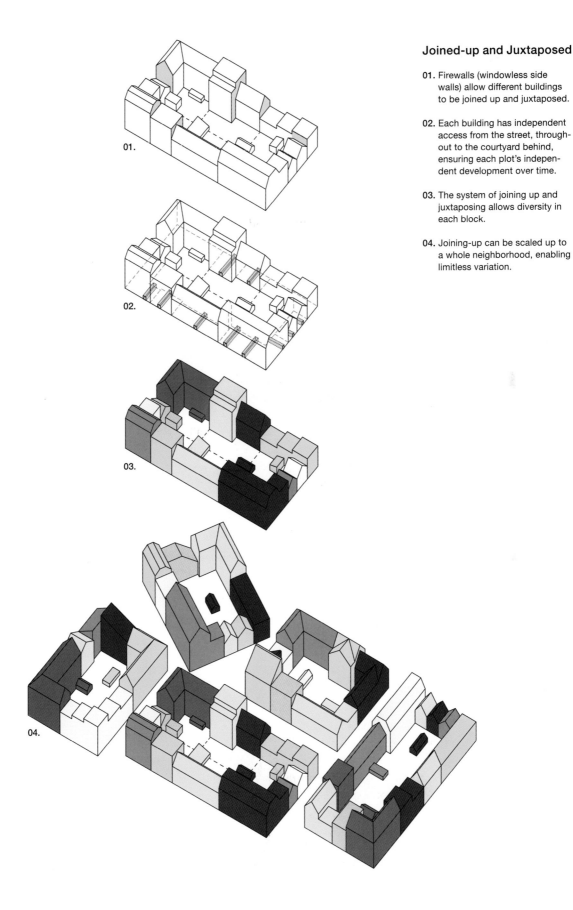

01.

02.

03.

04.

Joined-up and Juxtaposed

01. Firewalls (windowless side walls) allow different buildings to be joined up and juxtaposed.

02. Each building has independent access from the street, through-out to the courtyard behind, ensuring each plot's indepen-dent development over time.

03. The system of joining up and juxtaposing allows diversity in each block.

04. Joining-up can be scaled up to a whole neighborhood, enabling limitless variation.

01.

02.

03.

04.

01. **Temple Bar, Dublin, Ireland.** Architecture from different periods juxtaposed on the same street.

02. **Berne, Switzerland.** Old and new buildings, different uses juxtaposed in the joined-up pattern of building.

03./04. **Berlin, Germany.** Joined-up old and new buildings, juxtaposing different uses and users, as well as different architectural styles.

05.-08. **Copenhagen, Denmark and Melbourne, Australia.** Examples of accommodating the very small in a dense, urban environment. The smallness radically reduces the scale and interestingly becomes an attractive focus for human activity.

05.

06.

07.

08.

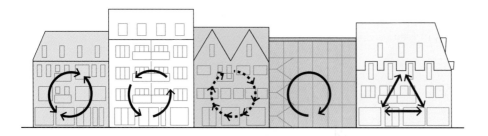

The independence of each building allows change, reuse, and renewal to happen in different levels over time. This means that, over longer periods, even greater social and economic diversity can coexist.

Some may allow change of use—for example, from dwelling to workspace or the other way round. Some buildings may be run for the highest possible profit, and others for no profit at all.

What is important is that there are not only different kinds of buildings, but that they accommodate different uses and different types of people in close proximity. Mixing old and new buildings can contribute to the socio-economic diversity described by Jane Jacobs.[7]

The diversity of use and users can contribute to a sense of community and make the neighborhood safer. A mixture of dwellings, workplaces, businesses, and services will ensure that there are people on a block at all hours. Different kinds of residents and users are at home and awake at different times of the day, which is particularly important for crime prevention.

Kugurazaka-dori, Tokyo, Japan. Characteristic narrow plots front the street, juxtaposing different buildings from different periods. The diversity of the ownership is reflected in an impressive diversity of the activities on the street. Offering something for everyone, this diversity makes the street the backbone of the neighborhood. Collage: Sotaro Miyatake

Another benefit of this pattern is that it accommodates small buildings. The inclusion of very small buildings radically changes the feel of a place, giving density a human scale and making room for varied activities that can add vitality.

Joined-up Buildings and Functions in a New Development: Caroline von Humboltsweg/Oberwallstrasse, Berlin, Germany

One of three reconstructed city blocks, this one—mainly made up of narrow-fronted townhouses along with a few tenement blocks—demonstrates the potential of the subdivision.

Described by Karsten Pålsson as a "modern Medieval city," every building here is independent from the other. Some have mixed uses, combining shops and offices on the lower floors with dwellings above; others are purely residential. All have front doors to the street and small, private gardens to the rear.[8] Also worthy of note is the deeper plan on the lower stories, acknowledging the greater value and potential of these floors. Combining both very attractive private and highly individualized situations for living and working, this block makes for a more lively public realm and more interesting pedestrian experience, showcasing a variety of comtemporary architecture.

Delivering Diversity in the Same Place:
Vauban, Freiburg, Germany

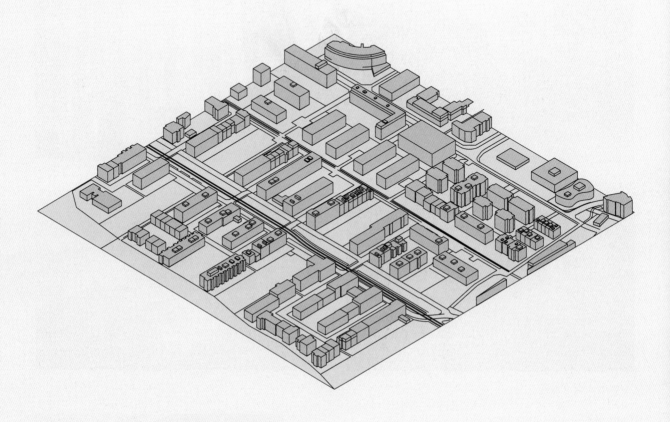

Build Density

Total area:	400 x 400 m/ 1,300 x 1,300 feet
Total floor area:	129,400 m²/1,394,200 sq. ft
Housing floor area (gross):	34,900 m²/375,300 sq. ft
Gross floor area ratio:	0.8
Site coverage ratio:	0.22

Ground Access

Build area with ground-floor access:	27%
Build area within ground-floor walking distance (4th floor or below):	80%

Types of Ownership

Private:	9%
Baugruppen:	57%
Cooperative oriented developers:	10%
Private developers:	26%

Already by 2002, a study of 450 homes identified the success of mixing a diversity of residents: 60% owners and 40% renters; 25% workers, 55% management level, 20% professional and self-employed; 10% single parents, 25% childless couples, 65% families with children; 75% having moved from Freiburg, 25% from elsewhere.

Freiburg, Germany, is a city known for its progressive investment in innovative public spaces, solar power, and cycling infrastructure. It has probably become the best known for its "Baugemeinschaft" cooperative building programs. New developments at Rieselfeld and Vauban stand out as exceptional in delivering new neighborhoods with high-quality housing in lively places with a distinctly urban feel.

Rieselfeld was the first, where the city of Freiburg prepared a seemingly conventional masterplan with townhouses and apartment buildings around protected courtyards, with clear fronts and backs, and a human scale. The plan had a stated aspiration of "children being able to play in green spaces, shouting distance from their parents." Vauban soon followed, on a former French military base in the inner suburbs of Freiburg. The plan was developed by the City of Freiburg, with support of the Green Party and participation from a variety of local grassroots groups.

The plan was a plot-by-plot development, guided by the Baugemeinschaft group as well as some private developers, to ensure the diversity of potential buyers. As with Rieselfeld, plots were smaller than the norm to encourage smaller-scale projects. Multiple parties might bid on the same plot, and the highest bid was not the deciding factor. In a role of stewardship, the City gave the Baugemeinschaft group priority over conventional developers when affordability, diversity of residents, and use of renewable materials and energy-efficiency were better demonstrated.

There was a strong desire to ensure that the new neighborhood was economically and socially diverse, reflecting the stability and vitality found in older parts of the city. Working with the motto "to give everyone a chance," the City considered each buyer for its "block profile," positively rating diversity of age, occupation, marital status, number of children, previous address, location of current workplace, and type of resident (owner or tenant).

There was a strong sense of place from the start. The new plan preserved almost all of the large trees, as well as most of the existing buildings, while the squatters in

01.

02.

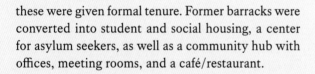

03.

04.

these were given formal tenure. Former barracks were converted into student and social housing, a center for asylum seekers, as well as a community hub with offices, meeting rooms, and a café/restaurant.

The plan is centered at the axis of Vaubanallee—a green, east-west running spine that also accommodates a tram line. The wide, grassy surface in the center muffles the sound of the tram and includes a stormwater swale. Vaubanallee is at right angles to Merzhauserstrasse, the main road that leads to the center of Freiburg. There is a natural hub of activity where these two streets meet. This is where the school and many businesses are located, as well as the hotel, which brings visitors into the neighborhood.

On Vaubanallee, there are many non-residential activities, including a kindergarten on the ground floor of an apartment building, shops, cafés, offices, and beauty salons. Looping off each side of Vaubanallee are U-shaped neighborhood streets, which are almost traffic-free with no street parking. The buildings are all

"walk-up" height, at three to five stories (net density of 95 units/ha), both apartment buildings and town-houses, many with mixed uses. Although the blocks are not completely enclosed, there is a clear pattern of enclosure, with recognizable fronts and backs, with buildings having a public, street-facing front and a more private, garden-facing back.

The simple devices of firewalls and separate entrances create a street of joined-up buildings. Every building is different, not just in terms of external appearance, with distinct architectural styles, different colors, materials, and details, but different sizes, standards, and apartment layouts. The diversity of types attracts people with different tastes and lifestyles.

This diversity makes for visual interest and promotes public life, facilitating orientation and making walking more rewarding. The diversity also makes for identity and pride, both for individual homes and for the community having a distinct and recognizable neighborhood.

05.

The different buildings present many different interpretations of active ground floors. There are plenty of doors to the street, front gardens, edge zones, shop-style windows, small business units, as well as outside stairs and access galleries, which are also focused toward the street.

The plan offers a variety of outdoor spaces, including private gardens in direct connection to the ground-floor rooms, and generous balconies, decks, loggias, terraces, and roof gardens. The gardens are shared with neighbors, and common outdoor spaces are shared with the wider neighborhood. There are larger public spaces, such as a plaza outside the community building and a forested landscape to the south, with a small stream.

The streets are important public spaces for playing and meeting. Although not car-free, Vauban promotes car-free living, with excellent public transport and bicycle infrastructure. Parking is accommodated in multi-story garages located on the edge of the district.

Vauban represents the combination of an ambitious plan by the City and enthusiastic and dedicated local activism. The development successfully accommodates greater density and diversity at a human scale with buildings oriented toward the public realm. The medium scale offers more opportunities for sociability.

By consciously creating smaller fractals, building by building, the Vauban plan creates tight groupings of households with a strong sense of identity, and nurtures community. It offers a viable, sustainable, and attractive alternative to car-based, suburban living.

01. An active ground floor, the bakery is a community focal point.

02. A green spine. Tracks in grass to help absorb the noise of the tram. Stormwater swale to the right.

03. Juxtaposed buildings. Different typologies, dimensions, and styles.

04. Side street as a shared space, with continuous sidewalks at end.

05. Different building architectures reflect the need for individual expression while shared outdoors spaces express the need for community.

The Baugruppen/ Baugemeinschaft Model

Far-sighted German planners predicted that a coming generation of young people would not be able to afford the high cost of developer-led property. In the last 15 years, German cities including Freiburg, Tübingen, Hamburg, and Berlin have developed cooperative building programs called "Baugemeinschaft" or "Baugruppen." This is a development model that allows the future owners to become the developers. By developing buildings individually, plot by plot, a diverse, high-quality, and more affordable building stock is possible. The Baugemeinschaft approach bridges the individual and private needs of residents and their common and social needs.

Seldom do urban dwellings respond to the needs of an active and growing family. Often, the only way to have a home designed to your own specification, is to find a site outside of the city and build a detached house. Designing your own home in an urban setting is often only an option for the wealthy. New apartments offer some choices, but they are limited to things such as bathroom tiles and kitchen cabinets. The idea of being able to influence the design of your own urban home, including the dimensions, layout, heating system, and insulation is extremely interesting.

The Baugemeinschaft sites are master-planned by the local authority and subdivided into small plots, which are then offered for sale at a fixed market price. The local authority will release a brief to interested buyers that includes height limits, allowable building density, inclusion of non-residential functions such as work spaces, range of dwelling types, mix of tenure types, and standards for insulation, renewable materials, and environmental performance. Generally, private individuals seem much more interested in innovation in housing than market-led developers.

The Baugemeinschaft offers a different investment model than conventional speculative development. There is less risk for the mortgage lender because the buyers are known from the very start. They are real people with names and addresses and financial security. Even if one or two people drop out or someone loses their job, it is not going to cause a project to fail.

Baugemeinschaft apartment buildings in Tübingen, Germany.

This kind of bespoke solution can be 40% cheaper than conventional, standardized housing since there is no profit for the developer.[9] The savings are realized because the Baugemeinschaft is the developer, and there are no marketing costs since everything is already sold from the start. The future residents often invest in better-quality materials and fittings and better technological solutions, which may reduce maintenance and running costs. It is unlikely that a speculative developer with only a short-term stake would make these kind of choices.

The spirit of neighborhood is present from the start of the project. The members of the Baugemeinschaft essentially choose each other as neighbors from the start. In the process of planning and building, they get to know each other and have the option to leave the project if they should fall out with each other. By the time the building is finished, the neighbors know each other well and the business of everyday coexistence can start. The Baugemeinschaft model produces buildings that are better tuned to the needs and aspirations of their residents. Residents are more likely to take care of the building and have a sense of attachment. This is the foundation of a stable community. With the long-term commitment to their project, they are more likely to invest in their surrounding neighborhood. The model is now being tested in other countries in Europe, and as far away as Australia.

A society is made of different people with different needs, different means, and different dreams.

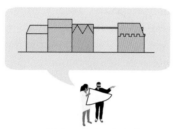

The city proposes a plot-based plan that allows many individual projects.

The Baugemeinschaft. Each group works together to develop the design and schedule for their own project.

The result is a diverse townscape with a strong identity, with buildings tailor-made to their users.

Layering

There is a vital difference between layering and stacking. Layering places different functions and types of accommodation on top of one another, and makes the most of distinctions between each space. Stacking merely places the same functions and the same type of accommodation on top of one another. Ideally, urban buildings should have clear horizontal layers, changing in character as they go up from the street level toward the roof as access and light conditions differ from floor to floor. The layered building accentuates these differences.

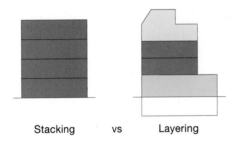

Stacking   vs   Layering

In the layered building, you can walk into the ground-floor level without having to climb stairs. Often, you can see straight into the ground-floor windows from the street—which might be an advantage, or might not, depending on the use. The ground floor can be extended at any time to have a larger floor surface, unlike the floors above.

The second floor has the convenience of close physical contact with the ground, while affording privacy and a sense of security, which traditionally earned it the name *piano nobile*. Moving up, the floors are subtly different from the ground floor in terms of accessibility, relationship to the ground plane, and daylight.

The top floor, attic level, or penthouse can take light in from above as well as from the sides. Often, the plan layout of the accommodation can be quite different since the walls are not necessarily load-bearing.

In the context of the enclosed block, there is also a vertical layering. Front-facing rooms that open onto the street differ from those that face the courtyard; courtyard buildings are different from those on the street; outbuildings are different from the main buildings; the courtyard is very different in character from the public street.

01. **Lille, France.** A multi-functional building with distinct layers addresses the urban location with shop units on the ground floor, office space in the middle, and penthouse housing units on the top.

02. **Tübingen, Germany.** An apartment building makes the most of the ground floor with a long rear extension with a generous terrace garden on the roof. The top floor apartments have a different plan layout than those below.

01.

02.

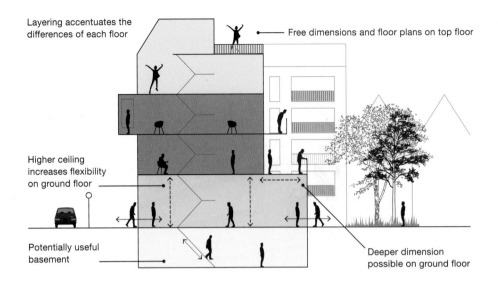

Layering accentuates the differences of each floor

Free dimensions and floor plans on top floor

Higher ceiling increases flexibility on ground floor

Potentially useful basement

Deeper dimension possible on ground floor

Layering on both planes creates a complex system of spaces indoors and outdoors. The more complex the spatial system, the more varied its qualities, the greater the chance that a variety of activities and behaviors will occur. There are several key factors in this complex system, including access arrangements, degree of exposure (public versus private), level of natural light and ventilation, dimensions and volumes, and, of course, room shapes and plan layouts.

Because both the ground floor and the top floor have distinct characteristics that are otherwise found in detached buildings, they are potentially more useful and more flexible than other parts of the building. Both of these can accommodate more diverse uses and users.

The enclosed, medium-height building is more likely to benefit from layering than a taller building, as it has proportionally more ground floor and top floor. When ground and top floor are combined, they may make up to half of the total built volume. This could mean that half of the accommodation could have useful characteristics normally associated with detached buildings. This is hugely significant in a dense, urban setting.

01. **Copenhagen, Denmark.** The so-called Amager Sandwich has three distinct layers with a supermarket on the ground floor, sports facilities in the middle, and penthouse apartments on the roof.

02. **Malmö, Sweden.** Layered accommodation at the Ohboy bicycle hotel. Guest rooms on the ground floor open directly to the street, bringing much activity with comings and goings to the street. There are different kinds of apartments above.

01.

02.

Layering Near Transit:
Nightingale 1, Melbourne, Australia

Photo: Peter Clarke

Nightingale 1 is a flagship project, an Australian iteration of a Baugemeinschaft type of housing, where the future residents take an active part in the development. Conveniently located next to a railway station and tram and bus lines, affordability was key in this project, Nightingale 1 aims to be environmentally, socially, and economically sustainable. The process of delivering Nightingale 1 generally gets all the attention, but the layered design of the twenty-first-century apartment building is also worthy of note.

The ground floor contains space for a café, an architectural studio, and an office space. These uses give life to the street throughout the day and create a kind of micro-community to come home to. Also on the ground floor is walk-straight-in cycle parking, a function typically located somewhere inconvenient. This is also an important detail as Nightingale 1 has no automobile parking spaces. At the front, life spills out onto the sidewalk with planting and seating.

Comfortably away from the ground, the middle contains four floors of apartments connected by a generous open stairwell, which also provides ventilation. (Nightingale 1 has no air-conditioning.) By cleverly exposing utilities, higher ceilings have been possible, which are hugely significant for light and the feeling of space in the compact apartments. The rooftop, with views over the surroundings, is a celebration of common uses with a lawn, summer and winter decks, a barbeque, sandbox, vegetable gardens and beehives, as well as a shared laundry and clotheslines.

There are already ongoing plans for the creation of Nightingale Village, which is made up of seven similar projects also located in Brunswick.

Layering in a New Development:
Nya Hovås, Gothenburg, Sweden

On what had been dismissed as leftover land beside a highway, the new development at Nya Hovås, south of Gothenburg, Sweden, is evolving into a thriving urban center. The process began by breathing life into some redundant light-industrial buildings with a broad range of uses, including retail, services, and recreation. The next phase introduced streets and courtyards in a traditional urban layout, as well as the new landmark, multi-purpose Spektrum Building.

Recognizing that mixed-use development was key in attracting people to move into higher-density areas, the developer invested strategically in ground-floor spaces for non-residential uses. Buildings with active frontages were deliberately placed along a busy route with heavy motorized traffic. The developer coached new businesses in the development, cultivating professionalism and helping with interior decoration and marketing.

The new urban blocks of Nya Hovås display classic layering, with business premises on the ground floor, facing the busy main street, and apartments on the floors above. Special apartments on the top floor make for a distinctive and varied roofscape, which adds character to the new neighborhood and makes a local landmark for passing traffic.

A Layered Building Accommodating Multiple Functions: Spektrumhuset, Nya Hovås, Gothenburg, Sweden

The Spektrum Building, the centerpiece of the Nya Hovås urban neighborhood, covers a full block and has active frontages on all four sides. The building takes full advantage of layering with bowling in the basement, a restaurant and shops on the ground floor, two levels of school classrooms, and a playground and co-working penthouse and roof terrace on the top.

The Spektrum building shows how one thoughtfully designed building can contain many different uses and, at the same time, activate its edges toward the surrounding streets.

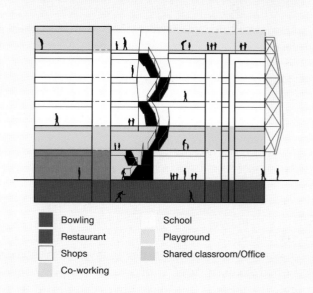

■ Bowling	School
■ Restaurant	Playground
□ Shops	Shared classroom/Office
Co-working	

Accommodating Different Functions by Layering:
Mercat de la Concepció, Barcelona, Spain

01.

02.

03.

04.

A successful example of a large building integrating into a mixed-use neighborhood, thanks to layering, is the modernized Mercat de la Concepció, a market hall in Barcelona. The historic market building has been preserved and renovated with a new supermarket, large loading dock, and carpark in a multi-level basement.

The conscious layering of functions has activated the market hall at ground level, allowing the many small traders—with their many labor-intensive and time-consuming activities—to enjoy the natural light and air and high ceilings of the historical space while connecting to the surrounding streets. Rather than presenting a closed facade, flower shops are located toward the main street, with their wares spilling out onto the sidewalk, bringing sensory delight and the flexibility to have longer opening hours than the interior market stalls.

There is a high density of employment at the market stalls, with as many as four or five people working in an area as small as 15-20 m² (162-215 square feet). Stools are provided in the market hall for the comfort of market customers who spend time carefully choosing their purchases and enjoying conversations with stall holders. It is appropriate that the busy and intensive life of the market is prioritized for more people to enjoy the sensory experience of all the produce in an environment (with natural light and ventilation) more conducive to staying and talking.

The market also houses a café bar, frequented by both stallholders and customers, as well as a hairdresser and a shop selling electrical goods. Below the ground-floor market is a supermarket with a large floor surface, stacked with more-mundane products. Here, there are only a few employees as the check-

05.

outs are thoughtfully placed up at ground level, with the cashiers well-treated like other stallholders, in the pleasant light conditions upstairs.

The market offers density and a diversity of products and experiences in the same building, well-connected to the surrounding neighborhood. The human experience—with practical walk-straight-in access and an active ground floor—is prioritized over the logistics of goods, vehicle deliveries, and parked cars.

The Mercat de la Concepció is not just about the co-location of different and complementary uses in one place. The market demonstrates the appropriate positioning of the different components, using layering, to prioritize the human experience.

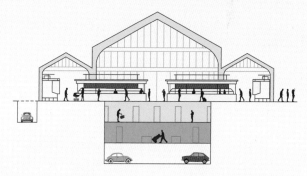

The market is organized into layers: the food hall is at ground level, above the supermarket, which is above the store, which is, in turn, above the car park.

01. Market hall on ground floor.
02. Flower sellers spill out onto sidewalk outside.
03. Side entrance connecting directly into neighborhood side street.
04. The small stalls can have 4-5 staff each.
05. Entrance bridging over supermarket in basement.

The Potential of the Ground Floor

A strong part of the case for smaller, enclosed blocks is the greater proportion of ground floors that they create. Ground floors—especially if they have a generous ceiling height—are more flexible than other floors, and in this way, can be more useful in accommodating density and diversity.

The active ground floor can accommodate a greater diversity of uses and ensure that more people spend more time at street level, connected to the life going on outside. Active ground floors can help to foster a sense of community and security, with more windows looking onto the street, and direct access resulting in more frequent comings and goings. The greater diversity of uses results in an activated space throughout the day. Ground floors support active mobility by making walking more interesting and making multi-tasking possible, as more services and goods are available as part of our daily movement patterns. Active ground floors are not to be thought of only as shops. On the contrary, active ground floors are just as significant for housing, workspaces, and other service functions.[10]

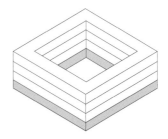

With a four- to five-story block, there can be at least 20-25% ground floor.

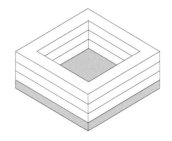

There can also be up to 100% ground floor without losing the integrity of the block.

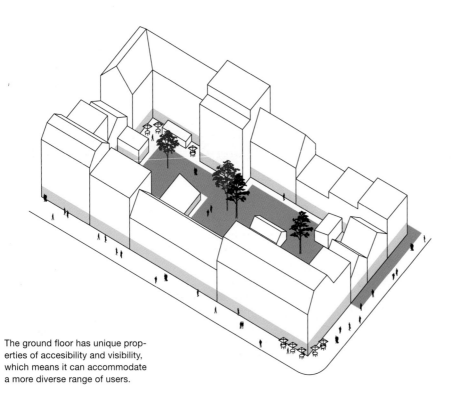

The ground floor has unique properties of accesibility and visibility, which means it can accommodate a more diverse range of users.

01.

02.

03.

04.

05.

06.

01. **Bellagio, Italy.** The value of what is visible at eye level has led to shopkeepers creating extra shop windows hung on the facade wall to maximize their commercial exposure.

03. **London, England.** The value of the ground floor has led to the extension of these modest townhouses with ground-floor shop units. Note that all of the attention (color, detail, and decoration) is concentrated on the first 3 meters/10 feet, what is experienced at eye level, while the buildings above with apartments remain rather plain.

05. **Tokyo, Japan.** Large windows on the ground floor connect people inside to those outside, helping build local community relationships.

02. **Tokyo, Japan.** Even modest, everyday workspaces can contribute life to the street. Here, workers at a family-run shirtmaker present their skills to the street, entertaining passersby while also attracting new customers.

04. **Edinburgh, Scotland.** The ground floor can accommodate many small, useful shops and services. The variation also makes walking around more interesting.

06. **São Paulo, Brazil.** A former shop unit has been converted into a community facility. The large windows inform passersby of what's going on inside, invite them to watch, and perhaps even step inside to participate.

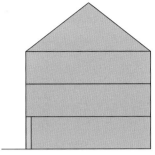

XS 25-60 cm/10-24 inches

XS

The smallest dimension for an active ground floor is 25-60 cm (10-24 inches) in depth, the size of a shelf or cupboard. This size would support very small businesses where the owner or vendor is outdoors. The dimension allows for the storage of goods and a display. A thoughtfully placed, built-in bench might also be considered an active edge.

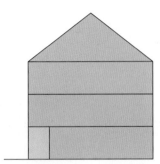

S 1-2 m/3.2-6.5 feet

S

A space 1-2 meters (3-6 feet) in depth allows the trader or shop-keeper to be inside, but generally does not accommodate customers. There could be a hole-in-the-wall-type opening to serve customers, who would remain outside. This could be a coffee stand, shoe repair shop, or a newspaper kiosk. This kind of unit efficiently uses the street as the sales space, as people queue up outside on the sidewalk. Frequently, goods will also be displayed outside. This kind of small unit is useful for lining larger, less-active ground-floor uses such as supermarkets or parking.

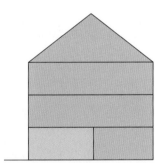

M 4-6 m/13-20 feet

M

A medium space, 4-6 meters (13-20 feet) in depth, can accommodate a small shop or office with room for customers inside. It is often situated on the front half of the building, toward the street. This could accommodate a whole range of small shops, workshops, and offices.

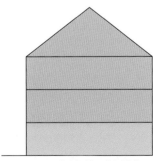

L 10-12 m/33-39 feet

L

A large space is one that fills the depth and width of the building ground floor. The public space, such as the sales floor or restaurant dining area, may extend all the way back. Alternatively, the premises may be divided up into zones, with sales at the front, storage and other facilities in the (darker) middle, and the kitchen, office, and staff space at the quieter back. For certain types of retail, "narrow frontage and deep plan" is preferred, and when repeated side by side, this form results in a dense and diverse street of shops.

XS The smallest dimension can allow the storage and display of goods.

XS: Belgrade, Serbia. A street shop made up of a thin layer of wall cupboards, where both shopkeeper and customers are on the pavement.

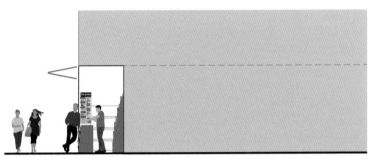

S The next smallest allows the trader to be inside while the customers stay outside.

S: Tokyo, Japan. Just a couple of meters allow this business to exist. Note the tiny windowsill bar and folding table.

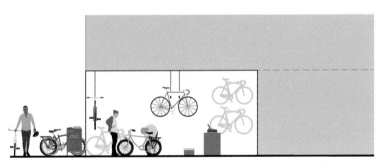

M The medium premises only address the street side of the building.

M: Copenhagen, Denmark. Single-sided shop units can bring more life to the street as they might have wider frontages.

L The large premises go from the front to the back of the building.

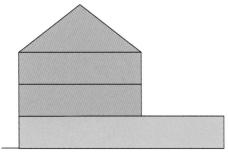

XL

In some cases, the ground floor premises might be deeper that the floors above, creating an extra-large and more useful space for certain functions (especially retail) that require a larger floorplate. Also, the larger ground floor can create a useful deck or outdoor space for the accommodation above.

XL 12-20 m/39-65 feet

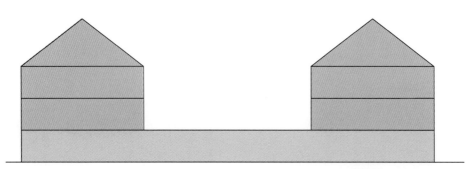

XXL 20+m/65+feet

XXL: The extra-extra-large premises can fill a whole block...

XXL

The ground floor premises may fill the whole surface of the ground floor, creating a podium courtyard level above. This extra-extra-large solution could allow a very large use such as a supermarket to move into a built-up neighborhood. The key is to wrap most of the outer edge with other smaller uses to create a continuous streetscape for better walkability and connection to the surrounding neighborhood. The podium creates a raised outdoor space, directly connected to the surrounding floors.

XL The extra-large premises extend beyond the width of the building.

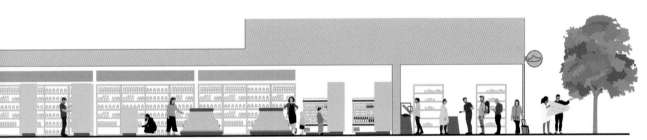

…with small shops on the edges.

XXL: Berne, Switzerland. A large coop-erative supermarket has been discreetly landed in a street by edging with useful smaller retail units. The otherwise boring facades are now more interesting for passersby. Having the bakery and ice-cream stand on the outside catches more potential customers and saves them time since they do not have to go into the bigger store.

Onto the Street

The most flexible space for business expansion is the sidewalk. Different size sidewalks and different uses can be combined with an active outdoor edge zone, which can soften the relationship with the street, encouraging people to linger. Particularly for the smaller units, this extra space is important. It can be used for anything from displaying goods, like crates of fresh fruit outside of a grocer's, or a rack of garments on sale outside a clothes shop, to accommodating tables and chairs for eating and drinking outside.

Spreading into the street is particularly important for restaurants and cafés in good weather, because apart from generating significant street life, this is when they can have their greatest turnover. The sidewalk or public space offers the potential to dramatically increase the area of a restaurant or café for a very low cost, both in initial, material investment of tables and chairs and also in maintenance, since cleaning outdoor space is much easier. Additionally, outside space requires no ventilation and is (generally) unheated. Perhaps more than any other ground-floor phenomenon, tables and chairs on the sidewalk generate more life on a street and contribute to a more diverse and higher-density use of urban space.

Even in residential areas, the sidewalk can offer extra living space. The presence of the residents, as well as their private possessions, in the public realm can bring an intimacy and conviviality to the street.

01. **Tokyo, Japan.** The small restaurant more than doubles its capacity when it spills out into the street space. Note also the plastic climate curtain on the neighboring restaurant.

01.

02.

03.

04.

05.

06.

07.

02. **Amsterdam, Netherlands.** Personalization of the edge in front of townhouses with a mini-garden of potted plants. This gives as much pleasure to the passersby as to the residents themselves.

04. **Helsingborg, Sweden.** Folding chairs on a sunny edge outside an ice-cream kiosk allow seasonal inhabitation of the sidewalk.

06. **Berne, Switzerland.** Thanks to a generous awning and potted plants, an outdoor room is created for the ground-floor café.

03. **Copenhagen, Denmark.** The appropriation of the narrow space in front of their dwellings gives the residents extra living space and connects them with the public space.

05. **Rinkeby, Sweden.** Combining a display table with hanging under a cloth awning, the shopkeepers spread right onto the street, creating a soft commercial edge to the pedestrian promenade.

07. **Edinburgh Scotland.** A basement café spills out first into the small, submerged forecourt, and then up onto the sidewalk.

More Than Just Shops:
Different Kinds of Active Ground Floors

Family Home

For a family with children, it is very convenient to live on the ground floor. A small garden, apart from acting as a buffer to the street, can be a valuable breathing space, a spot for storing bicycles, toys, or a pram, as well as a play space for small children.

Special Needs Home

This could be for an older person or a person with disabilities, where ground-floor access is extremely practical. The opportunity to get in and out unassisted enables connection with the world outside. Spending time outdoors, watching and engaging with passersby, gives the ground-floor resident the opportunity to build up a stronger relationship with their neighborhood.

Office Own-Door

The ground floor is a suitable location for an independent workspace. The street location offers visibility as well as social connection. You can step outside and feel part of the community. The presence of someone working on the ground floor brings life to the street and adds to the feeling of security.

Workshop

Ground floors can be used as workshop and studio spaces for creating, making, and repairing. The ground-floor space can allow artists, artisans, tradesmen, and craftsmen to be better connected to the everyday life of their communities. The street location is useful not only for customers visiting, but also for deliveries to and collections from these premises.

Childcare

The ground floor offers the advantages for walk-straight-in access and a "shop window" for institutional activities: day-care facilities and nursery schools, branch libraries, public services, community offices, and charity projects. Rather than being in isolated public buildings, these activities can be located closer to their users—as part of the street and as part of the community.

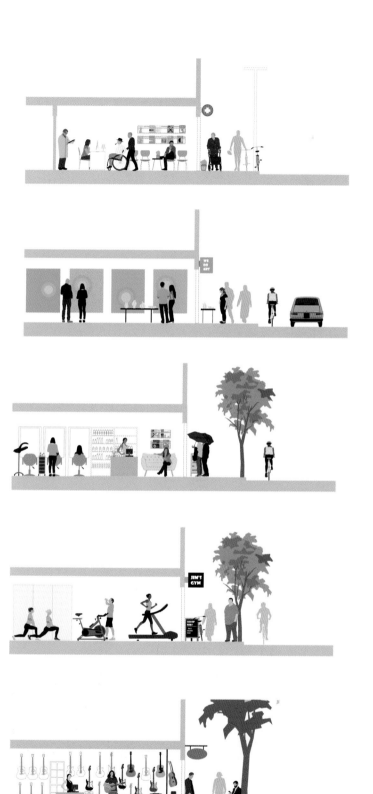

Healthcare

The ground floor can ideally accommodate the office for a doctor or dentist, a vet, or premises for any other specialist or therapist. For any visitor, it is easy to find and access because there is a street address. There is also the convenience of connection to other useful stuff, like the bus stop when arriving by public transport.

Showroom/Gallery Space

Larger surfaces of ground floors can also find life as showrooms and exhibition spaces. These might employ relatively few people per square meter but can still activate quieter side streets. The urban location, rather than a suburban one, makes such spaces and activities more accessible to more people.

Salon

The premises for the hairdresser, the beautician, the nail salon, and the barbershop deserve special attention because of the more sociable nature of their activities. The street windows look straight in on the activities, which makes the customers part of the display and makes these places feel livelier. The appointment system means they are equally busy throughout the day.

Fitness

The gym can occupy a large surface of a ground floor and brings life to the street with the gym-goers themselves, the best advertisement for the activities inside. Often open from early in the morning to late at night, ground-floor gyms put more eyes on the street and bring a sense of security to the public spaces outside, especially at times when other businesses are closed.

The Specialist Shop

Small specialist shops can bring life to quieter streets. Whether it's wool, model railways, secondhand books, or home-brewing, the window display is particularly important when the shop sells unusual goods. Specialist shops might have the majority of their sales online. However, a physical shop gives the opportunity for the business owner/shopkeeper to be part of a community and its everyday life.

The Value of the Top Floor and the Roof

In the same way that the enclosed block delivers proportionally more ground floor, it also delivers proportionally more top floor or penthouse compared to a free-standing or high-rise building. In a building with 4-5 stories, 20-25% of all the building area can be top floor. Like the ground floor, the top floor and the roof have particular characteristics that can benefit the user. By exploiting these characteristics, the performance and value of the building can increase. In the case of the top floor, the particular advantages are the unrestricted floor plan and roof shape, easy access to the roof surface, room for extension, as well as better views, more daylight, and natural ventilation.

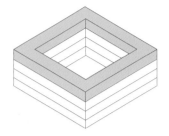

At 4-5 stories, 20-25% of a building can have the unique penthouse attributes of the top floor.

The top floor has the benefit of far greater freedom in the plan layout, regardless of what is below, because none of the internal walls need to be load-bearing. This plan flexibility can also allow for accessible "walk straight out" outdoor spaces on the surface of the roof. The volume of the top floor can have almost any form as there is nothing above. This allows for different roof shapes and varying ceiling heights, even in the same apartment, with the potential for double-height spaces as well as mezzanines. Additionally, the flexibility of roof volume can allow room for growth, with the possibility to extend upwards. Small, yet-significant, additions can increase functional flexibility and allow for greater customization.

The top floor is often perceived as being more attractive, as there is no one living above, hence the premium prices for penthouses. In many cities loft conversions are particularly popular as luxury dwellings, such as penthouse flats. The top floor has the potential to have many of the qualities of a suburban house, such as privacy, light, and private outdoor space. The flexibility of the top floor increases the likelihood that a different use or user could inhabit the top floor, increasing the social-economic diversity and dynamic of the building. However, in many situations, the top floor is an unexploited asset, with considerable untapped potential.

01. **Shoreditch, London, England.** A new, multi-level penthouse on an existing building accommodates duplex hotel suites with a rooftop restaurant and terrace above.

02. **Mexico City, Mexico.** New rooftop apartments enjoy the light of big windows and the space of roof terraces.

01.

02.

Living in the Roof:
Tööiö Housing, Helsinki, Finland

How do you integrate a taller building into lower surroundings? The answer might be a big roof. The giant and somewhat playful mansard roof of Tööiö Housing accommodates four floors of apartments, and somehow makes the eight-story building feel significantly lower. The use of the roofing material on the upper floors is part of the illusion.

The aerodynamic shape of the roof deflects the wind upward, protecting the courtyard space, while the angle of the roof lets the sunlight reach the courtyard floor. The roof's playful appearance, with the exaggerated chimneys, gives the place a friendly character. The small size of the apartments is compensated with protruding glass-box balconies, which make the most of the roof shape opening up to the big sky.

Although only one floor can be the top floor, the generous roof of Tööio Housing gives many apartments a penthouse feeling. The sloping roof windows let in more light than normal vertical windows and the balconies feel spacious and enjoy a 270-degree view.

50% of the height is in the roof.

The Value of Ancillary Space

Ancillary spaces—such as basements, attics, and rear extensions—as well as out-buildings—such as garages and bike sheds—provide room for growth and change over time.

In the short-to-medium term, attics, basements, and outbuildings can help accommodate many practical secondary uses, like seasonal storage, shared facilities such as laundries, hobby space, and protected bike storage. These are important functions that are often only found in a suburban context.

In the medium term, these simple buildings or spaces can be affordable premises for small businesses. These modest spaces can facilitate new enterprises in established and popular areas, with attractive neighbors and the footfall of potential customers.

The basement connected to the street might accommodate a newly started shop, while an outbuilding in a quiet courtyard might be suitable for a workshop for a maker or an office for a start-up. The presence of non-residential uses in a residential area adds to the resilience of the neighborhood by diversifying the population and increasing the likelihood of activity at all times of the day.

In the longer term, as the neighborhood location becomes more popular, these secondary spaces may become more valuable. There may be an opportunity to invest, converting and upgrading them into attractive living and working spaces. Former washhouses, stables, garages, and attics can become attractive homes. Mews houses and loft apartments are well-known examples of repurposing ancillary space.

01.

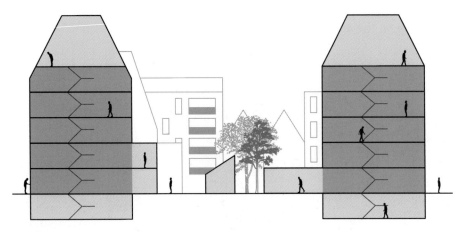

Attics, basements, rear extensions, and outbuildings all offer room for growth and new uses over time.

01. **Copenhagen, Denmark.** This former courtyard outbuilding has, over time, been recognized for its attractiveness—a little house in a quiet, protected courtyard directly connected to the amenities of the city.

02./03. **Breitenrain, Berne, Switzerland.** Outbuildings upgraded to high-quality office space in a quiet courtyard location ensure daytime life in the residential area.

04. **Copenhagen, Denmark.** On many sites throughout the city, former clothes-drying attics have been converted to top-floor apartments with exceptional views and light.

02.

03.

04.

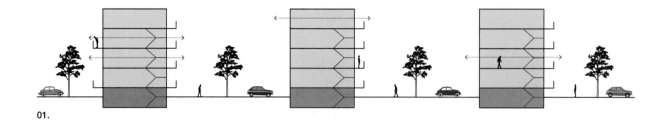

01.

Recognizing Spatial Diversity

If we make a simple comparison between a joined-up and layered building in an enclosed block and a stand-alone, stacked building in an open landscape—even if the stand-alone building has an unusual or eccentric architectural shape—the freestanding building generates fewer kinds of space than the one that is part of an enclosed urban block.

For a start, the stacked, freestanding building makes no differentiation between front and back. This means there is no public side, no apparent front where the main entrance might correspond to a street address. Nor is there any private side, no apparent back for the practical services any building needs—garbage cans, bikes, and the like. There is no busy side where a shop or service function might prosper, and no protected, quiet side suitable for children playing or sleeping with an open window.

Therefore, the freestanding building with its stacked accommodation might only have one kind of outdoor space and one or two kinds of indoor space. If we imagine there was a system for measuring spatial diversity—this building type could be given a *spatial diversity factor* of 2 or 3 since, inside and out, there are only two or three distinctly different kinds of space.

01. The freestanding, stacked buildings in an open landscape generate little spatial diversity. There are no clear fronts or backs and no obvious public and private realms. There is no real distinction in the experience of the different floors.

03. **Lund, Sweden.** The open plan with stand-alone buildings makes for a spatially monotonous environment over large areas.

03.

04.

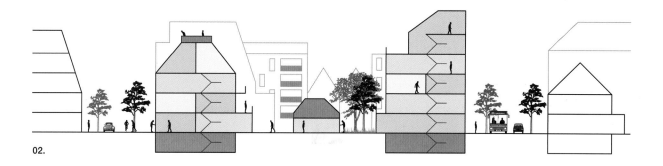

02.

02. The enclosed block with layered buildings offers considerable spatial diversity. The public space of the street is very different from the courtyard. Rooms facing the public front and private back are different in character. Being connected to the ground plane, the ground floor is quite different from the floors above.

A layered building that is part of an enclosed block can create more kinds of useful spaces than freestanding buildings in an open plan can create. The difference between the front/street and back/courtyard makes for at least two very different types of outdoor space. There may even be differences between adjoining courtyards, with a first or outer courtyard closer to the street, then an inner courtyard. There are certainly differences between rooms at the front or the back of the building or on different floors. The rooms that connect both front and back, are also different. Projecting extensions and outbuildings make for different kinds of spaces in themselves, while also creating different outdoor subspaces in between.

04./05./06. Copenhagen, Denmark. Enclosed blocks with layered buildings allow many different spatial conditions to exist in the same location. All three photographs are taken within 50 m (200 ft) of each other.

Using the same simple method as used above on the freestanding building, the layered block buildings with outbuildings could reasonably be said to have a *spatial diversity factor* of up to 12 or 13, thanks to its front and back conditions and the distinct layering from ground to attic. What is important is that each kind of different space increases the likelihood of different potential uses.

05.

06.

Accommodating Larger Elements While Maintaining the Human Scale

To make a neighborhood where living locally is possible, it is vital that there be easy access to work, medical and child care, learning, entertainment, and retail, ideally walking distance from dwellings. The buildings that house these uses are part of the density and diversity challenge. How do you accommodate a school, library, health and care facilities, a hotel, a cinema, a supermarket, or a company headquarters in a neighborhood? How do you accommodate larger uses in a neighborhood environment without losing the human scale? How do you ensure that these uses are connected to their surroundings at eye-level and are walkable?

Employment is probably the most important function as this needs to be accessed every day over long periods. A neighborhood should ideally provide a range of employment opportunities, including larger workplaces. Schools and daycare facilities probably come next, as they are used almost every day over several years. These facilities play a key role in neighborhood identity and meeting places, along with places of worship and other social and cultural institutions such as libraries and sports facilities, which might be used every week. Healthcare facilities, although they may not be needed every day or every week, are important throughout a lifetime. Everyday retail like supermarkets should also be integrated into the streetscape. However, there are particular challenges in accommodating buildings with uses that require very large surfaces in a way that makes them good neighbors to the medium-sized and smaller structures surrounding them. Clearly, some larger activities can fill an entire block, or at least a significant part of one. The larger buildings should be integrated into the local streetscape without breaking up the smaller-scale rhythm and life of local streets.

01. **Edinburgh, Scotland.** In a polite gesture, the mega-structure of the Victorian Balmoral Hotel (left) lifts its skirts to present small shops (unrelated to the hotel business) to the back steps leading to Edinburgh's main railway station, offering useful services to hurried passengers. The 1980s shopping mall (right) does not afford such courtesy.

02. **Barcelona, Spain.** A "mouse-hole" entrance to a chain supermarket allows the large floor plate of this function to be otherwise hidden while giving space to smaller local shops, offices, and residences.

01.

02.

03. Copenhagen, Denmark.
Illum department store. At five stories, this department store has a similar scale to the surrounding buildings in the medieval city center. Rather than courtyards, it has atrium spaces to light and ventilate the large floor plates and top floor with terraces and roof lights. Around the ground floor edge, the store is skirted by smaller flagship stores that bring more interest to the street.

04./05. Utrecht, Holland and Paris, France. A Protestant church and a Catholic Church. Two churches in different contexts, with small shops integrated along the edges, give more complete local environments.

03.

04.

05.

There is maybe something to learn from historical environments. In older towns and cities, larger buildings were integrated into smaller-scale places by softening the buildings both in terms of scale and use. A simple example is the traditional German Rathauskeller, literally the "town-hall basement," which is a restaurant and bar. The function is housed in one of the most important public and civic buildings. Importantly, this is not just a physical solution, where the restaurant softens the physical presence of the administrative building. This is also a socio-economic solution, inviting activity at different times of the day. The restaurant brings life to a central, civic location when it might otherwise be empty. Here a private, commercial, and popular activity co-locates with an official, public institution, allowing a private enterprise to generate income for the public administration. There are many types of public, civic, or sacred buildings with mundane and private uses in their basements or ground floors. These activities might be irrelevant (or even irreverent) to the activities of the main buildings, but in a way are also respectful to the continuity of the streets and life outside.

Large-scale Retail

Something as large as a department store can fit neatly into the scale of urban blocks of 4-6 stories. The courtyard spaces can be used as service yards that are invisible to the street. Atrium spaces can bring natural light into an otherwise deep plan and allow communication between floors. The larger function can host smaller ones, such as a department store hosting smaller shops around its edge, in a kind of economic symbiosis

The smaller shops help to attract customers to the bigger host, while also generating rental income for the host, which has higher overhead. The department store is a destination in its own right, and the smaller shops benefit from being in close proximity to this destination. The cluster of stores attracts a broad segment of the population and can offer a broad range of useful goods and services in a central location that is accessible on foot and open longer hours. The department store is also a major employer, providing a wide range of jobs.

The Loop of the Enclosure

The building block enclosure is continuous, creating one big loop. This loop offers multiple access options with no dead-ends. You can move endlessly in two different directions, making for flexibility of use. The loop can be subdivided into multiple components or be used as one large continuous space and is, therefore, capable of accommodating a broad range of uses—large, medium, or small.

The loop also makes servicing easy, allowing everything from cleaning carts and catering trolleys to electrical circuits and computer cables to move back and forth easily. For buildings with high service requirements, such as hospitals and hotels, this is extremely useful. Additionally, since the loop allows multiple access points, there are also many possibilities for evacuation in an emergency. For example, in the case of a fire, if one direction and exit is blocked you can turn around and go the other way.

Big Hotels in Small Neighborhoods

The reasons for locating a hotel in a neighborhood are many, for both hotel guests and locals. Hotel guests will be in a walkable location connected to other useful services. The hotel may have a symbiotic relationship with local businesses and will likely employ local people, with a range of higher- and lower-skilled jobs, often importantly employing young people and immigrants. The hotel's public spaces, such as the lobby—with comfortable seating, coffee, and internet service—can be useful, multipurpose places for meeting and working. These spaces usually have long opening hours, effectively 24-7, bringing an extra layer of life to the ground level and bringing a feeling of greater security to the neighborhood. By attracting a range of guests, from businesspeople to holiday travelers, solo travelers, families, and diverse groups, they generate an important customer base for local shops.

In an enclosed block, the continuous loop of rooms around a courtyard makes for efficient servicing. The courtyard form offers a choice of rooms—outside ones with city views and a genuine connection to the surrounding life in the city, or quieter inside rooms. The courtyard might be covered or partially covered for use as a large event space that requires large spans without columns. It could even become the main architectural attraction—the "wow" space of the building.

Maximizing the Potential of the Courtyard Block:
Radisson Blu Hotel, Berlin, Germany

01.

02.

03.

In one of the German capital's most central locations, the Radisson Blu Hotel maintains a discrete scale to emphasize the grandeur and height of the neighboring Berlin Cathedral. The lower heights make the hotel a good neighbor and allow guests to feel connected to their immediate surroundings.

The hotel building takes up a complete block, with a large indoor courtyard containing the hotel's bars and restaurants as well as a spectacular five-story fish tank, the world's largest. The tank is part of a major aquarium mainly housed in the basement. The building has an active ground floor, which brings life to the surrounding streets, with independent restaurants, cafés, and shops. The hotel takes advantage of the enclosed block with a loop for servicing and access/evacuation.

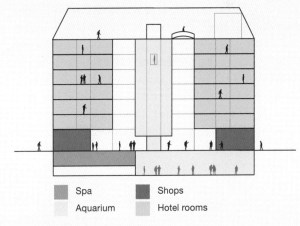

| Spa | Shops |
| Aquarium | Hotel rooms |

Section through hotel showing central atrium and aquarium tank.

01. Covered shopping street adjacent to hotel.
02. Discrete scale of large volume next to Cathedral.
03. Aquarium in atrium lobby.

Landing a Big-Box Megastructure in a Fine-grained Neighborhood: IKEA, Altona, Hamburg, Germany

In a time when online retail is increasing and large stores are pushed farther into suburban locations, the placement of a full-size IKEA store in a human-scale city neighborhood in Altona, Hamburg, Germany is a significant achievement. This size IKEA is usually found in a big, blue, industrial shed in the outer suburbs, next to the motorway. In the Altona neighborhood of Hamburg, it has been successfully inserted into a pedestrian street with small shops, businesses, offices, and apartments.

Unlike other IKEA stores, this one is accessible by public transport and on foot. The store demonstrates clear layering, with the showrooms on the floors near-est the ground and an active edge to the street with entrances, shop windows, the Swedish food shop, and an ice-cream café. The restaurant is one floor up, with views onto the street. The self-serve warehouse is located above the showrooms with car parking on the top floors.

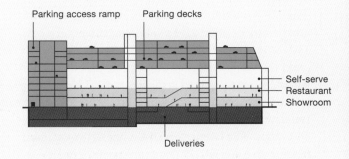

From Department Store to Workplace: Twitter Headquarters, San Francisco, California

For their headquarters in San Francisco, Twitter chose to move into a former department store on the centrally located Market Street. Large floor plates offer flexibility for ever-changing and evolving group-based project work, for collaboration and co-working as well as the relatively flat management structure of many companies. The abundant and open floor space on each level is vital for workers to meet each other for both formal and spontaneous encounters and exchanges.

An urban location is important, with easy access to public transport, walking, and cycling as well as shops and recreational and cultural amenities. The building mirrors its surroundings and offers amenities in its own right. The ground-floor level, with its big windows and shopfronts, has been maximized with attractive and useful functions, including cafés and restaurants,

a market hall, and supermarket, all inviting passersby to look in, come inside, look around, and linger.

The choice of the former department store on Market Street for this major employment hub tells us three important things: first, the kind of building that is needed for workplaces (large, flexible floorplates on fewer floors) and second, the kind of location that is necessary for attracting and retaining staff (centrally located, well connected, highly serviced). The third significant thing is Twitter's integration into the city with the generous ground floor with shops and services accessible to all—the public is invited inside the corporate property to hang out. Apart from the convenience for their own staff, having an authentic bit of city life inside their own building, Twitter has softened not only their physical presence but also their corporate image.

Layering High Density at a Human Scale:
Old Town, Berne, Switzerland

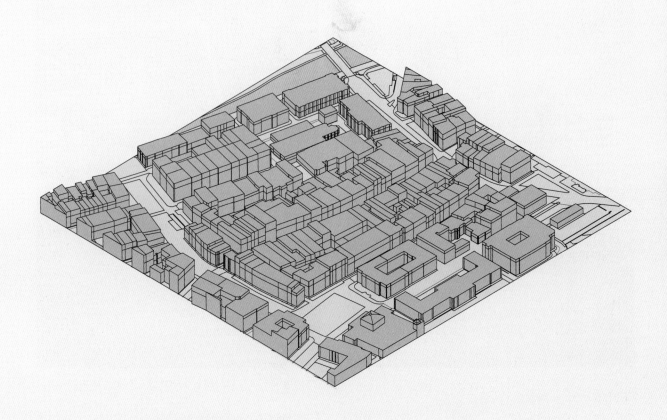

Build Density

Total area:	400 x 400 m/1,300 x 1,300 feet
Total floor area:	373,600 m²/4,047,200 sq. ft
Housing floor area (gross):	80,200 m²/864,000 sq. ft
Gross floor area ratio:	1.87
Site coverage ratio:	0.50

Ground Access

Build area with ground-floor access:	21.5%
Build area within ground-floor walking distance (4ᵗʰ floor or below):	62%

Berne Altstadt/Old Town

UNESCO World Heritage Site
0,85 km²/85 ha
4.600 inhabitants in the Altstadt
93 inhabitants/ha
140,600 inhabitants in the city
400,000 inhabitants in Greater Berne

The cross-section shows the relationship of the street with the arcades and public transport.

One of the best examples of density and a diversity of building types and uses at a human scale is in the medieval core of Berne, the capital of Switzerland. Berne's old town, especially around the central streets of Marktgasse, Kramgasse, and Gerechtigkeitsgasse, reveals the potential of diverse, dense blocks made up of medium-rise buildings. The streets are characterized by a mix of many uses and functions, resulting in a vibrant urban space. The use of these structures has changed over time, but the layout is essentially unchanged since its construction during the twelfth to the fifteenth centuries.

Simple Structures

The buildings are all four or five stories high, with big roofs and arcaded ground floors fronting the street, with courtyards to the back. The public side presents a consistent, ordered frontage to the street, while the private side with courtyards is more flexible, both in accommodating everyday use and also changing over time, allowing the buildings to expand inward without increasing their height or intruding into the public space.

The combination of the soft roofscape, the relatively low building heights, and the dense urban form makes for a pleasant microclimate between the buildings. The continuous, arcaded ground floor creates a promenade that can be used in all weather and invites people to walk, stop, stand, and linger. Narrow laneways reduce the size of the urban blocks, not only creating pedestrian shortcuts between the main streets, but also offering more shop frontage for commercial activities.

Accommodating Everyone and Everything

The Berne structure, with enclosed blocks at a human scale, can accommodate uses of almost any size, from extra-small to extra-extra-large, while maintaining its human scale. Extra-small might be a food stand or a flower seller in the shelter of the arcade, a stall on the market place, a kiosk tucked into a corner, or a tiny studio apartment in an attic, under the big roofs. Extra-extra-large could be a supermarket with an expansive floorplate, a department store, or a major hotel. In between is everything else: shops of all sizes, banks and showrooms, cafés, bars and restaurants, lawyers' offices, and medical practices. All of these coexist, enjoying the mutual benefits of proximity to one another.

There is a clear hierarchy in the spaces that helps accommodate the mix of retail activity. Chain stores and shops with a higher turnover obviously choose the main street, while smaller, privately run shops or those with a more limited clientele are in the lanes, back streets, and arcades. Varied historical ownership patterns mean that unlikely juxtapositions can occur, such as a small family business next door to a new international chain store.

The symbiotic relationship between activities on different scales can be seen in how the large entities, such as the supermarkets, fit in to the human-scale environment. Large retail units are enclosed by smaller shops on their exterior sides, so that the whole block remains dynamic and lively rather than being dominated by the monotonous, long exterior walls of one single function.

01.

Horizontal Layers

In Berne's central streets, there is very clear layering that starts with the most concentrated activity on the ground floor—the main, continuous retail level where shops thrive because they are easily accessed. This stretch of commercial space on the ground level sometimes extends one floor up or one floor down, depending on the needs of the trader. Occasionally, a shop may continue two or three stories up, as this allows the likes of department stores and furniture showrooms to exist in this location, alongside much smaller retailers and other uses.

Sometimes, thanks to outdoor staircases, the basements can operate independently from the ground floor. Since the rents are considerably lower for the basement spaces, they can offer start-ups or the more alternative traders access to prime, high-footfall locations. This layering enables different commercial subcultures, alternatives, and new businesses to coexist with conventional, established businesses. A shop selling used records might sit underneath an exclusive jeweler.

Above the ground-floor level, the buildings accommodate premises for services such as doctors and dentists, as well as all kinds of smaller offices for professionals such as lawyers, engineers, and architects whose visitors also benefit from the convenience of central location. A few residential apartments also remain. The ground-floor shopfronts are punctuated with doors to the staircases that lead up to the floors above, with signs and brass plates indicating the names and activities of the occupants. There are also banking premises at ground level, with complete office buildings above fitting into the blocks. For all of these, the conventional street layout means it is easy to find them by their street addresses.

From a client and customer perspective as well as that of the employee or resident, the co-location of numerous different activities makes for a very convenient, multifunctional environment. Everything is in walking distance, and you can do many different things in one trip.

01. The main street space.
02. A restaurant on a third floor podium catches sunshine that otherwise doesn't reach the ground floor of the courtyard. Note the proximity to the roof.
03. Some courtyards have been opened up to the public to provide additional retail spaces.
04. Temporary independent retail activity in arcade.
05. Nameplates demonstrate diversity of activities in the same building.
06. Temporary independent retail activity in arcade.
07. Pattern of shops in arcade and basement shops with independent access stairs.

02.

03.

04.

05.

06.

07.

This cross-section through street and buildings, shows the layering of different activities within buildings as well as the accommodation of larger and smaller functions.

Milch

Kosmetik

Kosmetik

SALE 30-50%

Reception

fika

Everyday Mobility

The central street accommodates a range of accessible mobility options. It is bicycle-friendly and has two-way tram and bus lines with arcaded promenades on each side of the tram tracks. The promenades are linked by easy pedestrian crossings, using the space between the two sets of tram tracks as an impromptu traffic island.

Delivery and service vehicles also have a place in the broader pattern of mobility. In order to respect Berne's UNESCO World Heritage status, many practical solutions have been found to accommodate modern service needs. In particular, lifts hidden in the pavements allow for deliveries to be made to the many retail outlets, including several supermarkets. This avoids the huge delivery bays and traffic geometry usually required for large trucks.

01./02. Lifts under the arcade floor and the pavement allow deliveries to the basements of the larger shops.
03. Trams and pedestrians comfortably share the same space.
04. With umbrellas the arcades offer a range of inside-outside experience.

01.

02.

03.

The Arcades

Berne's arcades offer a wider passage for mobility than the width of the street space itself. They create an extended comfort zone for walking and staying, bringing people closer to the weather without having to be out in it. They provide shade when the sun is hot and cover from the rain and snow. The arcades mean that the open skies are always just a step away, and you can be outside again the minute the rain stops. Restaurants and cafés have outdoor seating that can stay under the protection of the undercroft and can spill out into the street in good weather.

The arcades allow shops to display goods outside all year round. The columns add another dimension to this commercial activity, accommodating display cabinets and signage as well as affording the simple human dimension of something to lean on and sit against. The arcades are a significant hybrid space, softening the relationship between life inside and life outside.

The arcade offers a range of outdoor opportunities in different seasons.

04.

What an Enclosed Block Can Do

Typical Urban Block

A typical urban block of 4-5 stories. This particular urban form does much more than its modest appearance might first suggest.

Private/Public Space

The block system clearly defines public spaces at the fronts (or outside the block) and private space at the back (inside the block). Two very different worlds can coexist in extremely close proximity to each other.

High Density/Low Rise

The block system allows high-density development while retaining lower-rise, human scale, meaning people have closer contact with and easier access to the ground plane and the assets of the surrounding neighborhood.

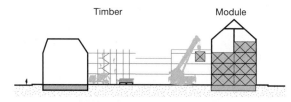

Simpler Construction and Foundations

Medium-rise buildings (4-5 stories), are more straightforward to build as they have simpler (and cheaper) foundations and construction systems compared with taller buildings. A broader range of materials (including timber) and different construction methods (including prefabricated modules) can be used, and smaller contractors and developers can participate.

Common Space and Identity

The enclosed block creates a common space in the middle of the block, which can be the shared focus of residents and a point for local community building.

Better Microclimate

The enclosed block creates a sheltered space, a protected microclimate, shelter from the prevailing winds, and a way to capture the sun as required. Consistent building heights reduce the negative effects of turbulent winds.

Protected Acoustic Space

The enclosed block creates a protected acoustic space. The surrounding wall of buildings shelters the inside space from the noise in the streets. This translates into sleeping with an open window in the summer and not being disturbed by traffic.

Protected Air Space

The enclosed block creates a protected air space, meaning that the air inside can be cleaner than outside in the streets full of traffic. This gives major advantages for ventilation, as well as everyday benefits like cleaner windows and hanging washing.

Protected Secure Zone

The enclosed block creates a protected secure zone, independent from the street, effectively a gated community in the middle of an urban, public context. This translates into a safe place to leave your bike and a safe place for your children to play.

20-25% Walk-In Access

In the enclosed block with 4-5 stories, 20-25% of the buildings have walk-straight-in access, a considerable benefit to a wide range of users and uses.

100% Walk-Up

The enclosed block with 4 stories has 100% walk-up access and the possibility of dual access to the public front and the private back.

Potential Development of Active Edges

With the enclosed block, it is possible to extend ground-floor activities (such as shops, cafés, and workplaces) up one floor to the first floor (+1) or down into the basement (-1). Ground-floor activities can also be extended back into the block. In this way, such street-related public activities can be doubled, tripled, or more without disturbing the inner world.

100% Vehicle Access and 100% Vehicle-Free

The enclosed block allows 100% vehicle access to all buildings on one side and 100% vehicle-free space on the other, offering the best of both worlds.

20-25% Penthouse

The 4-5 story enclosed block has 20-25% penthouse and valuable top-floor accommodation, which has the benefit of a free plan (as there are no load-bearing walls) and much more light as there can be windows in the roof as well as the walls. There is also the possibility to have roof terraces and roof gardens at a height where the microclimate is still pleasant. (Higher up exposure to stronger and colder winds can make outside spaces less pleasant and therefore less usable.)

Multi-Fractal System

The enclosed block can be subdivided into completely independent buildings, each with its own access, without losing its basic qualities. This allows for different architectural styles and different uses, as well as different ownerships and tenure types, to coexist as neighbors.

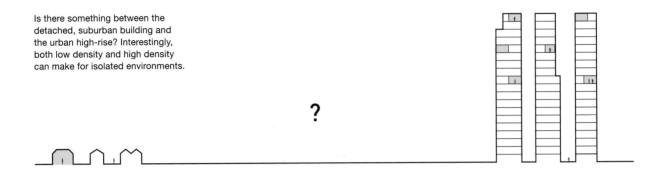

Is there something between the detached, suburban building and the urban high-rise? Interestingly, both low density and high density can make for isolated environments.

?

Building Blocks, Building Resilience

The urban pattern of enclosed blocks with independent, joined-up, and layered buildings can accommodate density and a diversity of uses while maintaining the human scale. This pattern can be repeated over and over again to allow cities to grow, adapt, and change over time. This urban pattern can combine both the comfort and security of the private realm and the convenience and accessibility of public life in a way that can improve everyday quality of life. The small, thoughtful details of scale open up opportunities for sociability. This is an extremely economical system in terms of space, material, energy, and time. Although many of the factors described may seem very basic, it is this very simple urban pattern of enclosed blocks, with its simple rules, that has created some of the world's most livable towns and cities. The seeming universal success of this building pattern makes it as relevant today as it has ever been.

It is the robustness of the urban framework of blocks that makes for resilience, accommodating the larger components of public life—department stores and supermarkets, schools and offices, institutions and sports facilities—alongside the small scale of private life, with its homes and gardens, workshops, and studios. This pattern makes the everyday easy: the public side of life with buying bread, walking the dog, eating lunch outside, listening to an entertainer, going to the market, goes comfortably alongside the private things like hanging washing outside to dry, having a barbeque, fixing your bike, playing in a paddling pool, packing a car for a trip, airing your bedclothes, and finding a sunny place for your tomato plants.

This simple system makes for a flexible framework that can be scaled up and combined. Blocks can be joined up to make streets; streets can be joined up to make neighborhoods; neighborhoods can be joined up to make whole towns and cities.

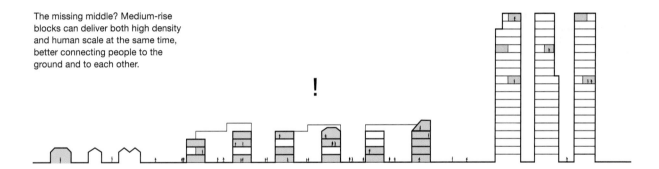

The missing middle? Medium-rise blocks can deliver both high density and human scale at the same time, better connecting people to the ground and to each other.

Together, you get a system of independent fractals with limitless permutations. Each individual building has the potential to adapt and change, in its own way and responding to the unique and specific circumstances of its users. The totality can make a resilient system, accommodating difference and tolerant to change over time.

This pattern of building might help us find the so-called missing middle in urban development in a time of rapid urbanization, when politics and market forces often demand densification. This "denser-lower" scale of medium-rise buildings, which creates both desirable public and private spaces, could both help deliver better new neighborhoods for the people moving into cities, as well as make good neighbors to the existing places and people already there. This is a density which can enable and support public infrastructure, public and private services, as well as recreational and cultural activities. At the same time, this is also a scale that responds to the particular needs and aspirations of the individual. This balance of common good and personal fulfillment might allow building blocks to build resilience.

Enclosure, joining up and layering can help deliver qualities that respond to our individual aspirations and needs—even at higher densities.

The Time
of Your Life

"Life is what happens to you while you're busy making other plans"

John Lennon, 1980[11]

The key difference between standard of living and quality of life, as I see it, is that standard of living comes down to the money we have and how we spend it, whereas quality of life is about the time we have and how we spend it. One is more about quantity; the other is more about quality. One is about stuff, and the other is about experience. Rather than finding ways of affording and accommodating more things into our lives, we might instead consider solutions to give us better ways of spending our precious time, lightening our load in life rather than burdening it, and helping change the daily stresses and conflicts of working, raising children, staying fit, shopping, running a home, and dealing with neighbors into everyday pleasures.

Perhaps the biggest challenge to living well is the physical separation of the different components of everyday life. Urban planning in the second half of the twentieth century hasn't helped this, separating and spreading different activities. It is hard to live locally when so many of the things we need and want are so spread out. The detached suburban house, the industrial estate, the out-of-town shopping center, the office park, the educational campus are all in different places. The dream of a peaceful suburban life, with the promise of a quiet, green, and safe environment, has the Achilles heel of requiring a car, which is both expensive to buy and to run. Not everyone can drive (e.g., children, the elderly, the sick, the nervous), and one household may have many different activities in different directions, so that one car might not be enough. What is more significant in terms of quality of life is not what the driving costs in terms of money or energy, but what it costs in terms of time.

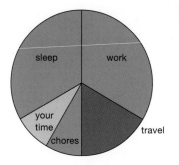

24 hours

Most people have to work at least eight hours a day, and if they are lucky, get eight hours sleep, leaving at the most eight hours for everything else, including daily chores. Travel time can eat up a significant proportion of this "everything else" time.

We waste so much time travelling between the needs and the wants, often missing out on other more fulfilling opportunities to better connect ourselves with the places and the people immediately around us. In the broadest terms, time is equitable and truly democratic because regardless of wealth, health, ethnicity, or education, everyone has just 24 hours a day in which to live their lives. After we have done all the things we have to do, what is left is the "everything else" time. This reflects directly on our quality of life, because the few precious hours left over every week is the time we have to spend on what we consider truly meaningful and worthwhile—investing in and advancing our lives, building relationships with friends and family, reading bedtime stories to our children, playing with the dog in the park, contributing to community life, learning and personal development (everything from home DIY projects to language classes), cultural experiences, starting a new business, volunteering for causes we care about, as well as all the other joyful, fun, and simple pleasures.

Can we design the physical environment of our cities and towns, neighborhoods, and streets to give us more time for the things that give us meaning? And can we make time more productive, or at least the passing of such time more comfortable and enjoyable?

The obvious way to change the current segmented paradigm is to co-locate more of the activities that make up our everyday lives, so we are living, working, learning, and relaxing in one place. This would greatly reduce or even eliminate the time spent in transit, which would also save energy and money. We would literally have several more hours a day to spend doing what we want.

24 hours

If you take the big chunk of travel time out of the equation, there is so much more quality time left for you every day, perhaps a few more hours to do what is meaningful to you.

Beyond having everything we need in closer proximity, we need to make the in-between times and in-between places more enjoyable and fulfilling. We need to make places that are loaded with opportunities to better connect us to where are, both in time and space, to unlock the real value of everyday life. For example, the trip to school might be family cycling time; the commute to work might be a pleasant walk through the park; lunch hour might become a chance for all kinds of multi-tasking opportunities and practical errands, even stopping at home or checking on your child at the kindergarten. The race to pick up the children from daycare would be less stressed, and there would be more time for after-school and after-work activities.

Imagine what you would do if you were given a few more hours every day. What would your day be like? It all comes down to how we build and use our towns and cities.

Getting About and Getting On

in a Congested and Segregated World

Walk up

Walk straight in

Wider sidewalks

Walk through

Median strip

Curb extensions

Congestion and segregation are related because the physical spread that comes with segregation requires more space, and this creates more traffic. The Modernist-planned city, with its separated zones and functions, creates a huge need for transportation to access the assets needed to live a full life.

At the same time, this physical separation makes for social segregation since different kinds of people and different activities are located in completely different places. Therefore, the zoned city not only makes for an inconvenient everyday life, it also makes for a social challenge as different groups of people (ethnic, economic, trade/professional, age) don't meet in a natural way.

Urban mobility is also about social mobility. The business of getting about connects you not just to where you are going, but also to the places you pass and the people you meet on the way.

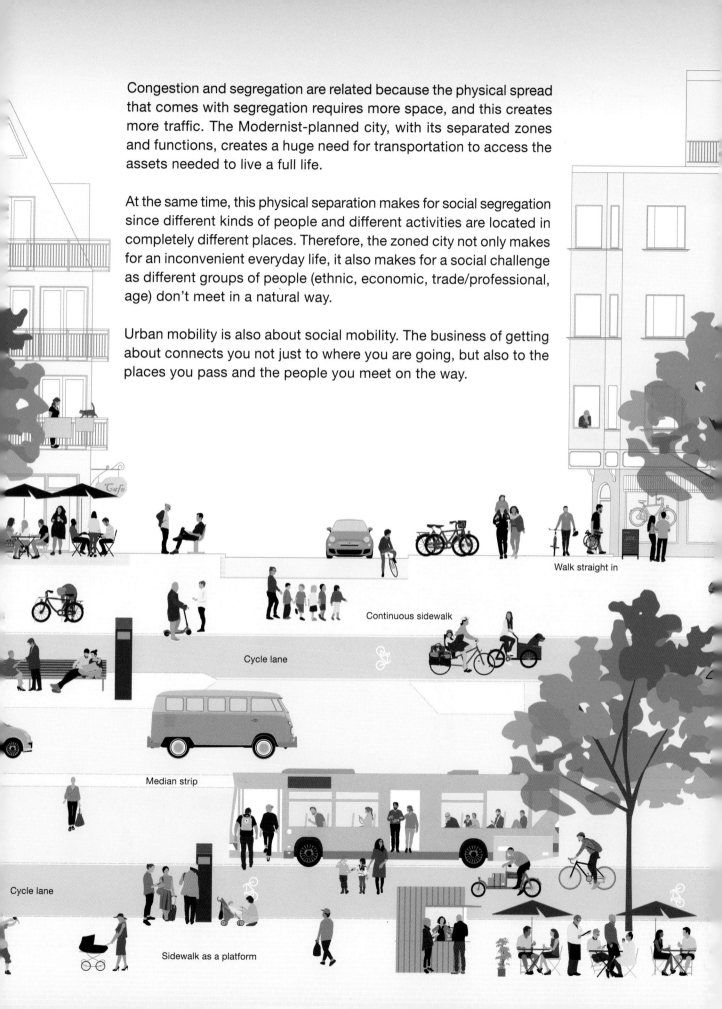

Walk straight in

Continuous sidewalk

Cycle lane

Median strip

Cycle lane

Sidewalk as a platform

The Human Dimension in Mobility

Within any urban system, no matter how well different activities are integrated locally, there is still a need for a range of mobility options. This starts with the smallest journeys, those from inside to outside—from your living room to your balcony, from your apartment door to the street, from your kitchen to the courtyard. These seemingly insignificant movements are vital to living a comfortable and convenient life. We might call this phenomenon *walkable buildings,* to be able to move from the comfort of the bedroom, bathroom, or balcony to the convenience of the bakery, bike lane, or bus stop in less than a minute.

Urban mobility includes walking, cycling, scooting, and public transportation, as well as private cars and all kinds of service and delivery vehicles. When we talk about this level of mobility, we might expect to discuss the relative benefits of different engineering and infrastructure systems, capacity, speed, and flow. However, there is another layer to mobility that is about the interface between the modes of transportation and people, and about how mobility systems, however large and complex, are integrated into the small scale of a neighborhood street. Like the walkable buildings, there are similar small movements around the neighborhood, for crossing the street, getting our bike onto the bike lane, and waiting for the bus. All of these small movements, using different forms of mobility, are opportunities for sociability—invitations for people to connect with other people.

01. **Basel, Switzerland.** A long-distance lightrail slows down to the people pace of the city center. The sureness of the rails means pedestrians feel comfortable to be close to the clean electric trams, which are much quieter than buses. Note the parked bike and the sleeping baby.

02. **Tokyo, Japan.** Users of all ages interact with different forms of mobility.

03. **Freiburg, Germany.** Public transport offers countless opportunities for encountering people who are different from you.

The human dimension in mobility starts inside buildings and seamlessly connects the different moments of everyday life.

01.

02.

03.

This is the human dimension in urban mobility. *Getting about* is a necessity of everyday life, while *getting on* is about making progress, advancing our lives, and connecting to and being comfortable with the other people around us. Walkability can make for sociability. We need to recognize that walkability is in every single step and every built relationship, in every building where people live and work, and in even the smallest spaces in which people move.

Walkable Buildings

At four or five stories, the enclosed urban block has a human scale, with buildings that are easily accessible (see Building Blocks chapter). This human scale makes social interaction easier. Most people can walk up three or four flights of stairs with relative ease, and at least up to the fourth floor, it is possible to maintain good connectivity with the street. From the fourth floor, you can observe what is going on and even engage with the life at street level: call in children who are playing in the courtyard, toss keys down to a friend, or call out to someone you know.

When designing major transportation infrastructure, there is the concept of creating a feeder system. Mobility planners are increasingly aware of the importance of the last mile (or last kilometer) traveled, from the station hub to home, for example. In the soft city, the aim is to take this mobility concept in a neighborhood even closer to the home, all the way into the building, into the stairwell, up the stairs, right up to the apartment door. The care taken in these last feet or meters is very significant for connecting life inside and out, and for the quality of the relationship between people and their neighborhood, its places, its people, and its climate.

Walkability starts at the door of your home and brings you out onto the street. Physical proximity and direct access to the street connects your private and personal life to the public life of the city. Walkability includes walk-in, walk-through, and walk-up buildings.

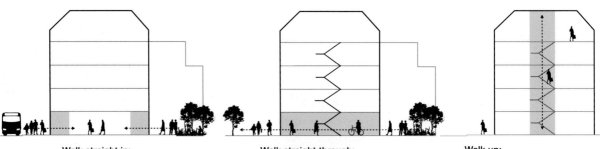

Walk straight in:
Convenient access.

Walk straight through:
Creates possibilities for diversity of uses in the same place—both public and private.

Walk up:
Easy acess to all upper floors and, for most people and situations, no dependence on an elevator.

Walk Straight In

The simplest and perhaps most important type of access is being able to walk straight in and walk straight out of a building. This is the real value of the ground floor, being immediately accessible to both the outside edge (to the street) and the inside edge (to the courtyard). The more windows and doors directly connecting inside and out there are, the better. An urban form with proportionally more ground floor can have more direct walk-straight-in situations, creating more opportunities to connect with other people, especially with immediate neighbors.

Walk-straight-in ground floors offer universal access, including for wheelchair users and others with disabilities and limited mobility. Walk-straight-in ground floors are very practical when carrying or moving things. For a home, it might be carrying in the daily or weekly shopping or carrying out the garbage, carrying children, strollers, and car seats, bicycles, luggage and sport equipment, and occasionally, furniture and appliances. For a business, there is the ease of clients and customers walking straight in, but also the convenience of easily receiving goods and disposing of waste every day. The better aligned the inside space is to the pavement outside, the more convenient the access.

Walk Straight Through

01. Tübingen, Germany.
   Walk straight in.

02./03. Copenhagen, Denmark.
   Walk straight in and walk
   straight through.

Walk-straight-through access, via a covered entrance passage or a connecting hallway, creates an ease of connection between the public realm of the street and the private world of the courtyard, getting from one world to a completely different one in a matter of seconds. Within an urban form where two such distinct kinds of outdoor space exist in such close proximity, the potential to walk straight through from private courtyards to the public realm is extremely convenient.

01.

02.

03.

Additionally, because the ground plane is the most accessible, it has the greatest potential to accommodate a diversity of uses. Therefore, the more independent the access is through the ground floor of the building, avoiding the private accommodation of the ground floor and the stairs to the upper floors, the greater number of different activities can potentially exist in the same location.

Both walk straight in and walk straight through, when combined with independent access to basement spaces from the street or from the courtyard, increase the opportunity for a greater diversity of use.

01.

02.

Walk Up

Perhaps the most significant aspect of walkability in denser built environments is being able to access all of the upper floors easily by stairs without being dependent on an elevator. There may well be an elevator for deliveries and to ensure universal access for those who really need it, but the stairs should be the primary connector to the upper floors.

Some basic details in design can significantly change the experience of using the stairs, such as natural light, ventilation, and views connecting to the outside. Having the stairs broken down into smaller sections, with a dog-leg staircase, for example, gives the user more opportunities to rest and makes climbing the stair feel less challenging.

The accessibility of the top floor is particularly interesting. As has been mentioned earlier, the top floor has many distinct benefits, including privacy, spatial flexibility, the big sky with abundant natural light and the possibility of private outdoor space—all qualities similar to a suburban, single-family house. With only three or four flights of stairs from the ground, all of these private advantages are in easy reach of the all of the public resources of the neighborhood just a minute away.

The Value of Walkable Buildings

Being able to move in and out spontaneously has a huge impact on quality of life, especially when living in an urban context. There are the immediate health benefits for individuals of having exercise, breathing fresh air, and having more social contact. But for the community as a whole, the feeling of neighborhood comes from people being present and active in and around the public spaces, with children easily getting out to play and adults engaging with their surroundings and their neighbors. Lower buildings, and especially housing at ground floors, make that more likely because it is simply quicker and easier to get in and out. With an average of four stories, 25% of the accommodation has direct access to the outside, potentially with their own door to the street. With an average of five stories the number is 20%. In the same way, 20-25% of the accommodation can have the penthouse advantages of the top floor. With medium height buildings of four to five floors, everyone can live within a minute's walk from the world outside.

01. **Copenhagen, Denmark.**The passage allows walk-through access from the front to the back of the building.

02. **Berlin, Germany.**

03. **Berlin, Germany.** The passage can also be combined with the staircase.

04. **Berne, Switzerland.** The secure staircase can allow for more informal behaviors.

03.

04.

Life on the Stairs

There is an enormous difference between a staircase and an elevator. Apart from the daily dose of exercise, common staircases can function as social forums, creating daily opportunities to encounter your neighbors. The stairwell is the backbone of the walk-up-height building. It has the potential to create a small community of next-door or near-door neighbors. With fewer stories, there are fewer households per level, which translates into more control and a more intimate situation. It is more likely you will recognize and get to know your neighbors in a walk-up building than in a high-rise building, because there are simply not as many people to get to know.

The sluice, which is created by the common stair, between the door to the street and the apartment door, is a valuable buffer zone between the private home and the city outside. In some ways, the stair is a miniature gated community, which creates a highly regulated and secure zone around the home. However, unlike suburban gated communities, this community is located in close proximity to the public world, so it is not isolated. In this way, the buffer of the common stair can help to mitigate many of the challenges of living in dense and diverse urban environment.

Take the stairs or wait for the elevator? With an urban form made up of lower buildings of four or five stories, a greater proportion is likely to be walk-up and the overall neighborhood will be more spontaneously accessible.

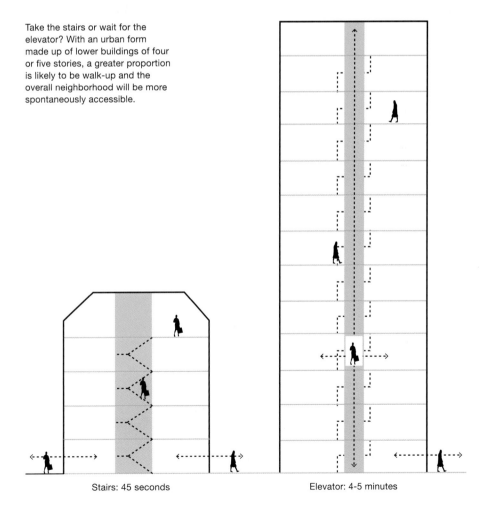

Stairs: 45 seconds   Elevator: 4-5 minutes

Accessing "Your Outside"

For every building, there is something that I call "your outside"—the piece of ground right outside your window: your bit of the sidewalk or grass, the place right outside your building. Your outside has the potential to become your piece of the community to engage in and maintain. If something happens here, you can do something about it—an accident, a crying child, anti-social behavior. Jane Jacobs wrote vividly about the street scenes she saw from her row-house window, and the vital role a street-watcher can have, such as making the street safer ("eyes on the street").[12] And while windows are eyes on the street, I would add that doors mean "arms and legs on the street." Windows are, of course, a vital component and frequently cited for crime prevention. However, doors onto the street send a stronger signal of security, warning would-be perpetrators and assuring potential victims, not only that you will be seen, but that you can be reached as well.

Snapshots by Jan Gehl from his classic lecture series, showing how people try to connect with "their outside" even when the architecture doesn't allow it.

It is a strange situation when there is a space right outside your window that you cannot access directly. Instead, you have to go to the other side of the building to find your way out and then come all the way around the outside of building to get to your outside, taking a few minutes rather than a few seconds. Perhaps, after all that effort, it does not feel very much like your outside.

It is vital to have access as close as possible to both the front and back sides of a building, immediately accessing public and private outdoors. There should be frequent stair cores with access to both the front and back doors. Ground-floor spaces should connect directly to the spaces outside their windows and upper-floor spaces should connect as immediately as possible to the spaces below their windows. Having immediate access to the street is what makes city life so attractive. The fact that you can get to so many different places in the span of just one minute is part of the beauty of urban life.

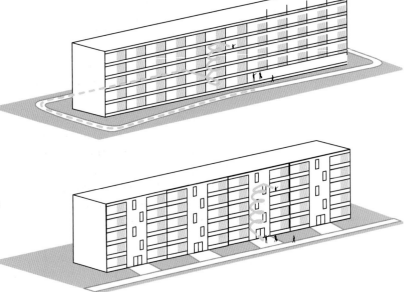

Accesing your outside in 4-5 minutes. Many Modernist buildings only have access to one side, meaning that residents cannot access "their outside" without a long detour. Internal corridor systems only make matters worse.

Accesing your outside in 45 seconds. There has to be a logical relationship between one's dwelling and the space just outside. There should be entrance doors on both sides of a building as well as frequent stairwells.

Making Streets

The most ancient traces of human life on Earth are paths. Networks of paths came long before buildings and urban blocks, marking the patterns of mobility and reflecting the economy of human energy: walking. The street as a space resulted from connecting these patterns of human mobility to the human activities in buildings.

When buildings are grouped along a route or around an open space, they create useful spaces such as streets and squares. These are part of the public realm, which makes identifiable spaces for movement and other outdoor activities. Historically, this was the most economical way to connect the maximum number of properties to the expensive infrastructure of a paved roadway, drainage, water, and other utilities as well as public transport. Connecting buildings directly to infrastructure gives private properties access to the public network and connects everywhere to everywhere else. In this way, there is a direct and dynamic connection between buildings and infrastructure, between the static world and the mobile world, between the private world and the public, between individual households and the larger urban population.

The public realm of places such as streets and squares can nurture citizenship by bringing people together and enabling them to spend more time outdoors, participating in public life. However, this can only work when the public realm is a predictable and comfortable place in which people know how to behave, what to expect, how to get around easily, and where to find the things they need. The pattern of streets and spaces between the blocks should create a relatively simple framework for movement. People can recognize the public realm and use its structure to instinctively navigate the town or city. Street and place names become addresses and corners become orientation points.

Having the buildings joined up saves space, requires less infrastructure, and allows different things to exist closer to one another, which is rather convenient when you are on foot. If there is less wasted space in between, you can get to more places faster by walking. The structure of the street also creates a commercial opportunity, with buildings connected to the flow of passing traffic. The edges of the buildings can be shopfronts, and by co-locating premises along the same street, shopping and business centers are created.

Corners

The pattern of streets between enclosed blocks creates corners: the more blocks, the more corners. We know that the greater the number of intersections, the more walkable a neighborhood is, as there are more choices of routes. In this way, the number of intersections has a direct influence on how much people walk, and the frequency of intersections is a barometer for health in urban areas.[13]

Corners are an extremely important element in street life. They are significant places, points for orientation, popular locations where people meet, and sites for commercial space. At ground level, corner buildings provide a highly visible location for shops, cafés, and other businesses. They can attract passing customers from different directions. Corner spaces on higher floors are also attractive due to the quality of light coming from two sides and the multidirectional views.

It might not be possible to have active ground floors on every street, especially in residential areas. However, whenever possible, there should be a ground-floor use on the corner that is relevant for the neighborhood, whether it is a commercial, institutional, or local community use.

01. **London, England.** The bright red shopfront stands out from the other white residential buildings, demonstrating the value of the corner location.

02. **Tokyo, Japan.** The tiny shop on the corner is, in fact, a corner shop within another corner shop, demonstrating the value of the location in a local neighborhood.

03. **Copenhagen, Denmark.** A new neighborhood with a café as an active corner. Note the diagonal cut on the corner is only at ground level, acknowledging the busy pedestrian movements where the streets meet, but retaining the efficient rectangular geometry above.

04. **Dublin, Ireland.** A classic corner shop, with its entrance door on the champfered corner, picks up footfall from two directions. The champfer here provides vital extra pavement space.

01.

02.

03.

04.

About Walking About

Jan Gehl frequently reminds us that human beings are biologically designed to walk.[14] Walkability is about accommodating walking, making it easy, efficient, and enjoyable. Walking will always be a vital component of urban life. It is the most essential and basic form of mobility. Every journey, regardless of the mode of transport, begins and ends with walking. You walk to the carpark or the bicycle shed; you walk to the bus stop; you walk to the metro platform. Walking is what makes all of the connections to the city possible, what connects us to the places in closest proximity, and what has the potential to get us beyond our immediate surroundings.

The pace of walking allows for a rich, sensory experience, promoting social interaction as well as connections to the surrounding environment. Urban spaces can be designed to enhance these experiences, improving overall walkability. This means creating comfortable, attractive, and continuous walking surfaces, and spaces that make it safe, easy, and intuitive for diverse groups of pedestrians to move among the other forms of traffic sharing the same spaces.

Unlike other forms of transport, people can have total control when walking—spontaneously stopping and going at will. Walking is the form of transport that is most responsive to what is going on around us and offers the most opportunities for connection. The short walks to connect to other modes of transport are particularly important.

If you drive straight into an underground garage from the street and then take a lift up to your home or office, you are denied the opportunity to connect with place, people, and planet. Simply separating the place for storing cars from the home or workplace with a small walk, apart from having some obvious health benefits, opens up the possibility of connecting. It offers a chance to see what is happening on your street, to see other people, and to feel the weather on your skin.

Different kinds of people walk in different ways, with different stuff. Designing for walkability must take into account the diversity of people walking and their circumstances. Some are in a rush to get their bus, where every second counts.

Others are strolling and looking for excuses to stop. Some people are actively engaging in exercise while others, like the postal carrier, are at work. Some will be wearing sensible walking shoes, while others will be in high heels or rubber boots. These different people with their different needs and different paces share the same sidewalk.

In the same way, there is also a range of urban equipment that people may have with them, allowing them to do more and be more comfortable as they move about the urban environment. The prams and strollers, shopping trolleys, walkers, wheeled suitcases, tote bags and shopping baskets, rucksacks, folding bicycles, headphones, mobile devices, water bottles, coffee cups, umbrellas and parasols all influence the way pedestrians move and use space. When we plan for walkability, we need to factor in this equipment and the accompanying behavior, and understand how it might help or hinder how people move and the space that they need.

01. **Basel, Switzerland.** Thousands of pedestrians share the same surface as twelve tram lines outside the Basel Central Station. Unlike bus lanes, the tram tracks provide intuitive guidance for exactly where to walk to be safe.

02. **Copenhagen, Denmark.** City-center sidewalks aren't always dimensioned for both walking and staying activities.

03. **Copenhagen, Denmark.** The sidewalk is used by many small wheels, including strollers and tiny bikes.

04. **Berne, Switzerland.** Sidewalks need to offer suitable surfaces and dimensions for wheelchairs.

01.

03.

02.

04.

Crossing the Street

One of the biggest challenges of walkability is simply crossing the street safely. This is when pedestrians truly meet their neighbors in traffic, and it is when the diversity of transportation can actually pose a threat to people walking. Sometimes, the location of pedestrian crossings is inconvenient or seems like a detour, which means that they are not always going to be where those on foot choose to cross the street. Getting across the street is particularly challenging for the youngest and oldest. As a child, crossing the street is probably the biggest obstacle for life in the city. Yet, it is a key to having a functioning everyday life.

Pedestrian footbridges and underground passages limit street-crossing options. They create isolated and sometimes disconcerting environments, while the stairs require considerably more physical energy from the pedestrian. They are also barriers to universal access.[15]

Corners pose a challenge for walkability because they are highly dense, busy, and complex. Intersections have the greatest concentration of traffic, pedestrian and vehicular, with everyone stopping and starting and potentially changing direction at the same spot. They pose the biggest threat to pedestrians because of the unpredictable nature of the other forms of traffic. We often see an increase in speed as vehicles rush to make it through the changing lights.

There are also informal sidewalk crossings such as vehicle entrances to garages or car parks or other interruptions where pedestrians share the sidewalk with motorists. These situations can confuse pedestrians because they always cannot predict or anticipate where traffic is coming from. Changes in level and surface materials, slopes, and curbs often benefit the vehicle rather than the pedestrian.

05.-07. Tokyo, Japan, Hong Kong, Melboune, Australia. Making it easy to cross the street is one the most essential details for urban mobility.

Similarly, walking surfaces can become cluttered with obstructions for pedestrians. This includes unnecessary curbs, poles, signs, infrastructure, utilities, and other objects on the sidewalk that might impede walkability. However, other people and their equipment can also be obstructions. If the sidewalk is simply not large enough to accommodate the number of people and diversity of uses, then walking can become stressful, irritating, and difficult. This is especially true for people with specific needs such as those walking with prams, strollers, walkers, or wheelchairs.

05.

06.

07.

What follows are some simple solutions to some of these challenges, with examples from cities around the world. What they have in common is that they are simple, low-tech solutions that are intuitive to use and make the pedestrian's life easier.

The Median

The pedestrian crossing with lights and painted stripes is a symbol of road safety. However, it is an inflexible and sometimes inconvenient solution to crossing the street on a frequent and everyday basis. It is important to create streets that meet the needs of a diverse population, with different desires and behaviors. People need to to be able to cross the street more spontaneously and conveniently than pedestrian crossings sometimes allow.

Adding a central median strip to a street can dramatically change how pedestrians coexist with vehicles. The median sends a signal to motorists that they are sharing the road with other types of users such as pedestrians and cyclists. This change can shift the way that everyone uses the space, and can alter the behavior, flow, and speed of traffic on the street. This creates an environment that promotes walkability as well as a culture of coexistence between pedestrians and vehicles as neighbors in traffic.

The median enables pedestrians to cross the street almost wherever and whenever they want with relative ease. They have fewer lanes to cross since they can negotiate the traffic coming from one direction at a time. The median is important because it directly addresses people's individual and immediate needs. The street becomes softer, and the atmosphere of the street as a whole changes for the better. When combined with cycle lanes in the street, there are additional stopping points for the pedestrian, making crossing the street even easier

A median strip can be functional in a variety of sizes and forms allowing for different kinds of movement. For example, it may have a curb to prevent certain movements, or be flush with the street to allow vehicles to easily cross over when needed. This is a way of controlling or limiting the movements of vehicle traffic. The dimensions can range from just a few cobblestones wide—just enough to accommodate the feet of a person standing—to large enough to accommodate other elements of street life such as trees or parking spaces for bicycles.

01. **Vesterbrogade, Copenhagen, Denmark.** The narrow median allows pedestrians to follow their desired path, spontaneously crossing the street, even if the traffic is only clear in one direction, as they can stop halfway until the other direction is clear.

02. **Kensington High Street, London City.** Apart from allowing easier and spontaneous crossing for pedestrians, the wide median also functions as a parking place for bicycles. This use and the frequent presence of people in the middle of the street has changed the culture of driving, and now there are less accidents since the median was introduced.

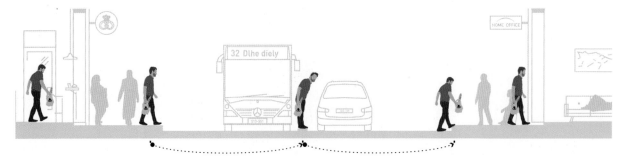

The median gives the pedestrian a safe haven halfway across the street, making crossing the street easier.

01.

02.

Continuous Sidewalks on Side Streets

In the hierarchy of urban streets, it makes sense to let the vehicle traffic flow uninterrupted along more-important streets, and have traffic stop and yield on more-minor or side streets. The same should be true for pedestrian traffic. Why should pedestrians on a main thoroughfare have to stop and wait at every single side street when the vehicles travelling in the same direction don't have to? Pedestrian crossings sometimes force those walking to make detours, throwing them off their natural direction or *desire line,* to allow for a road geometry based on the turning circle of large vehicles. Pedestrians often far outnumber vehicles in an urban setting. Who should be prioritized when designing the street?

Copenhagen, Denmark. One of the simplest and yet most significant details in the urban realm: continuing the pavement across the carriageway of a side street.

In London, Copenhagen, and other cities, walking is prioritized by designing the sidewalk as a continuous surface, to stretch over side streets. This effectively transforms several smaller blocks of sidewalk into a single, long block. Turning cars have to carefully negotiate their way across the sidewalk, observing and respecting the pedestrians, and always yielding to them.

Redesigned side-street crossings that prioritize the pedestrian alter the balance of who has the right-of-way in traffic. People on foot are favored because motorists come as guests in the pedestrian realm. The crossings are a simple change, but make a huge difference for pedestrians in terms of level of access, comfort, and safety on the sidewalk.

Other examples:
The continous pavement radically changes conditions in urban environments, taming car movements and allowing safer, smoother, and uninterrupted walking.

01. Frederiksberg, Denmark
02. Aalborg, Denmark
03. Copenhagen, Denmark
04. Lyon, France
05. London, England

The continuous sidewalk can eliminate frequent and annoying changes in level, which makes things easier for people using wheelchairs, prams, and strollers, wheeled luggage and shopping trolleys, scooters, and kick bikes. Overall, the continuous sidewalk creates a more comfortable, safe, and pleasurable experience for people walking. It is also faster since there is no time wasted waiting for traffic at side streets. The continuous sidewalk means that children can be more independent, exponentially expanding their everyday networks—walking to school, visiting friends, and performing errands are possible without adult supervision.
Having this safer mobility option can open up a whole new world of freedom, learning, and experience for a child, and can give free time back to their parents.

The continious sidewalk prioritizes pedestrians.

01.

02.

03.

04.

05.

The Curb Extension

Corners are neighborhood focal points. These small, local points of concentration where paths cross create many opportunities; street corners can be dedicated meeting places or just an opportunity to stop, take a breath, and observe the surroundings. However, corners and intersections can be challenging given the number of pedestrians moving in different directions and the crowding of people waiting to cross.

The curb extension at the corner is a simple yet highly effective solution to some of these challenges. It redistributes space in a more balanced way, with the pavement widening toward the intersection. It creates more room to accommodate pedestrians waiting to cross and their movements, better views for people looking about to orient themselves, and provides space for local activities relating to the social or commercial potential of the corner. The curb extension can tame dangerous driving behavior at the intersection while also making crossing distances shorter and safer for pedestrians. There may be space for street furniture, giving a moment of respite on an otherwise busy thoroughfare, and for planting in the otherwise hard landscape of the street.

01.

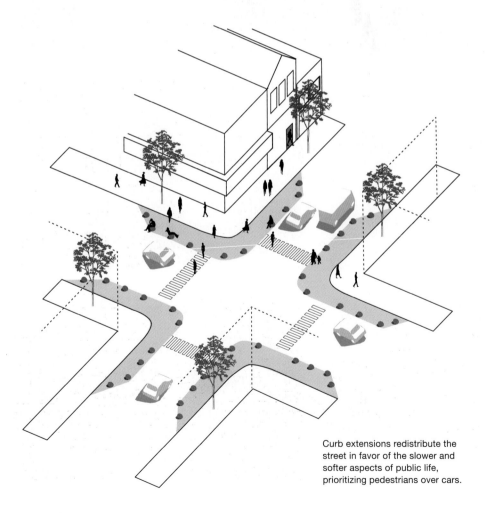

Curb extensions redistribute the street in favor of the slower and softer aspects of public life, prioritizing pedestrians over cars.

01./02. Lyon, France. Curb extensions at corners make crossing the street easier and can make space for parklet-style spaces furnished with chairs and tables.

03./04. Mar del Plata, Argentina. This pilot project extends curbs at corners using only paint and temporary bollards. An assortment of street furniture and planters invites people to stop, stay, and sit in the former car territory. Photos: Municipalidad de Mar del Plata

05./06. Buenos Aires, Argentina. Painted curb extensions make crossing the street easier and invite staying activities.

02.

03.

05.

04.

06.

The Sunny Side of the Street:
Vester Voldgade, Copenhagen, Denmark

In the Nordic countries, one of the simplest ways to change a street from a thoroughfare into a place where people want to stay is to make the sidewalk wider on the sunny side of the street. This offers pedestrians the opportunity to interact with the place and the other people, while also enjoying moments of better weather.

In Vester Voldgade, Copenhagen, the street has been redesigned and activities added in relation the functions nearby. For example, a ping-pong table has been placed near the school and space has been created for outdoor tables and chairs near cafés and restaurants.

Before

After

Much More than Just Walking

The street is perhaps the most significant public space as it is right outside your door. At the same time, streets often make up 30% of the open space in a town and city.[16] Perhaps the simplest improvement to walkability and to public life is having a wider sidewalk, giving more space to pedestrians, whether stopping, standing, or moving. A wider sidewalk makes for a climate of tolerance and greater comfort for a broader range of users—from people strolling aimlessly side by side to people rushing to get somewhere.

Most cities have plenty of data on motorized vehicles and almost none for pedestrian activity, leading to a bias toward the car in decisions on the distribution of space. Frequently, pedestrians are given proportionally much less space, even if they are, in fact, the largest user group. In a wider debate about what the street does, it can be argued that pedestrians improve the perception of security, help build community, and spend more money in local businesses. Passing cars cannot do these things in the same way.

There are other elements of the sidewalk that can support pedestrians and make walking around the city easy and accessible while, at the same time, developing public life. For example, having a bench or a chair is important both for supporting a diversity of pedestrians and offering a place to rest while walking, thus allowing people to walk further. The same public seating supports staying activities, inviting people to spend more time outdoors.

In a similar way, kiosks provide useful services, allowing people to stay longer in the public realm. In addition to creating meaningful jobs and potentially thriving businesses on tiny footprints, the presence of these kiosks on a street makes the public realm feel safer.

01./02. Melbourne, Australia (below left) and **Rio de Janeiro, Brazil** (below right). Kiosks in central districts bring a feeling of security to the streets in areas that otherwise lack nighttime population.

Spending more time in public spaces means that people are open to the spontaneity of the street. Staying, stopping, and sitting allow for social interaction, developing acquaintances, and building neighborhoods. People can decide to do things on the spur of the moment such as sit down to enjoy the sun shining, drink a cup of coffee, or simply take a break.

01.

02.

Integrating Cycling

Similar to walking, cycling is non-polluting and healthy, as well as an extremely convenient and sometimes pleasurable way to get around. Cycling is cheap and accessible to almost all. Since most everyday, local trips (daycare and school, grocery shopping, gym etc.) are relatively short, cycling can be a convenient and practical option.

Cycling can be an option for those who may have trouble walking longer distances, and also enables people to take more things with them than they could otherwise carry when walking. On a bicycle, you can transport your child, your pet, your shopping, sports equipment, and many other items. The benefit of the bicycle sharing the load is not to be underestimated.

Cyclists can adapt their routes with ease. You can get door to door seamlessly, at your own pace, and without needing a timetable or having to find a place to park. This accessibility comes at a very low cost. Cycling, after walking, is probably the most accessible form of transportation.

Cycling should be recognized as a part of everyday life. Moving about at eye level, cyclists have a similar perspective to pedestrians, and they also benefit from being part of the life of the street. On a bicycle, it is possible to stay connected to your surroundings—people, places, activities, and the forces nature—in a way that is more difficult on a bus or a tram and quite impossible in an automobile. Spontaneous interaction and participation in neighborhood life is easy; it takes only a few seconds to hop off your bike to greet a friend or stop in a shop. All of this makes getting around by bicycle more enjoyable.

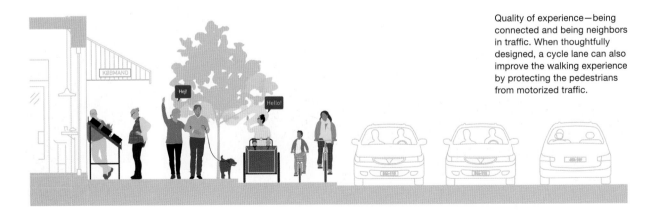

Quality of experience—being connected and being neighbors in traffic. When thoughtfully designed, a cycle lane can also improve the walking experience by protecting the pedestrians from motorized traffic.

Like pedestrians, cyclists come in many forms and have different abilities and behaviors. There are long-distance commuters and Lycra-clad racers alongside grandmothers and postal carriers. Bicycles come in different sizes, from tiny child-sized kick bikes to big cargo bikes. There are other small-wheeled phenomena like skateboards, roller skates, and kick scooters. Significant additions to this wheeled group include electric bikes and electric scooters. E-scooters, apart from being seen as great fun, lower the threshold for active mobility use, while e-bikes allow more people to travel farther, faster, in worse weather, and, importantly, uphill. All of these different users need to be accommodated into the street. The solution is to create dedicated cycle lanes for the soft mobility of the smaller, lighter wheels of bicycles, scooters, and skaters.

Different kinds of cyclists with different needs and different speeds.

01. São Paulo, Brazil
02. Luzern, Switzerland
03. Bordeaux, France
04. Tokyo, Japan

01.

03.

02.

04.

Safe Cycling for All:
Copenhagen Cycle Lanes

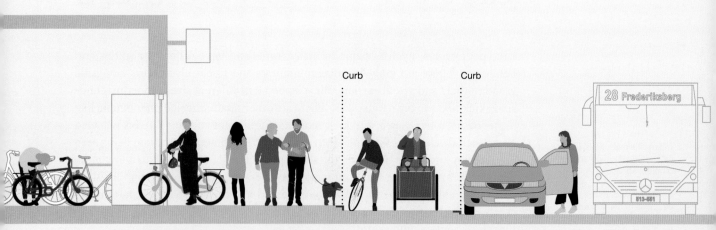

Curb   Curb

28 Frederiksberg

Cycling among motorized traffic in an urban context can be extremely challenging and potentially dangerous. Cyclists can feel vulnerable balanced on their delicate little bikes when surrounded by big, heavy, and fast-moving motor vehicles. The Copenhagen cycle lanes are undoubtedly a best practice in terms of integrated and soft bicycle mobility in an urban space. Lanes provide safety and comfort, making cycling much easier and more predictable. The cycling system is simple and easy to understand. The cyclists have their own space yet remain integrated with the life of the street and the other users.

The Copenhagen model has a dedicated cycle lane between the sidewalk and the motorized-vehicle lanes. The cycle lane is separated from the pedestrians with a low eight centimeter (3 inch) curb, enough to make the zones distinct. More importantly, there is a second curb of the same size that separates cyclists from motorists. Each mode of traffic has its own surface, which gives a simple sense of order as everyone knows their place. In the same way as people know that cars don't drive on the sidewalk, cars don't drive on the cycle lanes either, and cyclists don't cycle on the sidewalk. This clarity means that the most basic conflicts are avoided.

It is important to maintain consistency in the relationship between the sidewalk, cycle lane, and street. The cycle lanes are one-way. Intuitively, the cyclists move in the same direction as the motorized vehicles, so there is no threat of oncoming traffic, and the potentially fatal danger of collision is avoided. Because the cycle lanes are placed right next to the sidewalk, cyclists

01.

02.

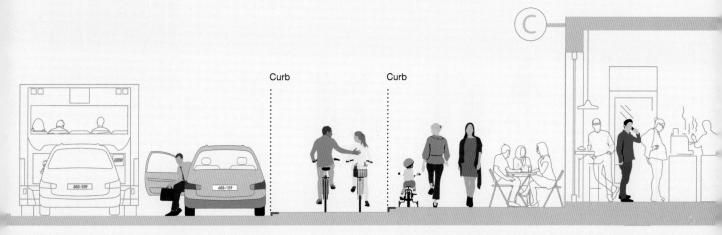

Curb   Curb

only have cars on one side of them, rather than cars on both sides, which can be common in other cities. The real perception of danger and stress for cyclists stems from the motorized vehicles on the road, not from the pedestrians. Having to deal with cars on only one side makes cycling feel much easier and safer.

With the Copenhagen model, parked cars act as a protective barrier between the cycle lane and the lane of vehicle traffic. In many cities, parked cars are placed between the sidewalk and cycle lane, which makes for a more complicated and stressful traffic situation for both cyclists and drivers. For motorists, parking in urban situations is already one of the most stressful aspects of driving without the complication of dealing with of cyclists. If motorists are forced to cross over the cycle lane to park, they must carefully maneuver

in and out of the space, often reversing with limited visibility, looking out for oncoming cyclists, which can be difficult and hold up traffic, and is particularly dangerous for the cyclist. Once parked, they also have to be sure that they do not catch a cyclist with their driver-side car door when exiting the car. By keeping the business of parking cars outside of the business of cycling, the Copenhagen model can been seen as a "win-win," allowing different types of mobility with different needs to coexist.

Another important benefit to the cyclist with the Copenhagen model is the ease of getting started. There is immediate access to the system since the lanes are conveniently located next to the sidewalk.

01.-04. **Copenhagen, Denmark.** Cycling in all seasons.

03.

04.

Paris, France. The Danish moment in Paris—spontaneous stopping is possible and attractive when the cycle lane is right next to the pavement and the shop fronts.

Since cyclists are so closely connected with the ground-edge pavement, they are able to take in what is happening on the street, and spontaneous stopping is easy. Designing the cycle lanes next to the sidewalk allows for a phenomenon that might be called *the Danish moment.* As you are cycling past the bakery in the morning and smell fresh-baked pastries, you can, on the spur of the moment, decide to jump off your bike and pick up a breakfast treat for yourself and colleagues on the way to work.

This ease of access to the ground edge also means that cyclists can be good customers for local businesses. They shop more often than car drivers because they can stop more spontaneously. It is important to understand this kind of behavior to address potential conflict between prioritizing cycle lanes over parking spaces outside shops. This ease of stopping also adds to the whole understanding of the neighborhood.

Cycle lanes should be able to accommodate at least two bicycles. It's much better if they can be three-bicycles-wide so that two cyclists can ride side by side, and other cyclists can easily get by. Recognizing that some cyclists travel faster than others helps to avoid conflict. There is also a huge value in allowing urban cycling to be a social opportunity. *Conversational cycling* allows friends or family members to cycle in parallel, sharing the experience of cycling and having valuable time together. The opportunity for parents to cycle parallel to their children is important, not just for having quality time together, but also to build up their child's confidence as the child learns to cycle in the urban environment.

Conversational cycling

Hybrid Cycling

Walking is easily combined with other means of transport, but combining cycling with other modes seems less obvious. However, when you do combine cycling with public transport you can achieve extremely fast and efficient trips. For example, when transit accommodates bikes, you can cycle to the railway station, bring your

01.

02.

01. **Montpellier, France.** The tram system accepts cycles on board, making for efficient combined trips.

02. **Copenhagen, Denmark.** All taxis are required to have a rack to carry at least two cycles.

bike on board, and then from your arrival station, cycle on to your final destination. Buses, trams, metros, and trains that allow you to bring your bike on board allow you to make longer trips that integrate cycling or even shorter trips when cycling might not otherwise make sense. Even taxis with bike racks can help you and your bike get home late at night, during a snowstorm, with a flat tire, or when you are simply too tired. When combined as a hybrid journey, these components make getting around the city exceptionally easy and convenient.

Hardware and Software

Designing for cycling requires both hardware and software. The hardware includes well-designed lanes, traffic lights to control traffic and maintain safety, ramps to help cyclists get up and down stairs with ease, foot rests to make stopping at lights easier, bike parking spaces to keep order, roofs and canopies on bike parking to keep cycles dry, facilities like air pumps and repair shops to help maintain cycles, racks on buses, trams, and trains that allow cyclists to bring their bikes on board to make long trips more convenient.

The software is equally important to developing a vibrant and secure cycling culture. Software includes data collection and research, communication and educational campaigns, cycle proficiency tests for school children, cycling classes for adults, awareness of local cycling norms (such as special hand signals), law enforcement and street maintenance (like plowing snow), as well as organizing events that unite and encourage all kinds of cyclists.

Cycling can be an extremely efficient, convenient, and positive form of active mobility. It is a simple and fast way for people to get around with flexibility, while affording people the chance to be part of the ground edge of the street, making social encounters with neighbors a natural part of the process. When incorporated thoughtfully into the streetscape, with accommodation for the density and diversity of cyclists, cycling can effectively coexist with other forms of traffic.

Street-Based Public Transport

Efficient public transport can reduce urban energy consumption and pollution. Beyond the environmental aspects, public transportation can play an important role in creating community and more-dynamic public life. Public transport offers important opportunities for people to be exposed to differences while sharing the same relatively confined space. Overhearing conversations and opinions on unfamiliar topics, seeing how other people behave and dress, as well as the simple, physical proximity to strangers, are all significant experiences in an otherwise segregated world.

People have more opportunities to experience and connect with their surroundings when moving along as part of the street. Walking and cycling are the most connected forms of mobility, as you are more exposed, but even inside a bus or a tram, you are moving at street-level, frequently stopping, seeing what's going on around you, and getting a sense of the actual distance. When traveling underground on a metro, spending time in a car focusing on the traffic, or even up in the air on a monorail, you don't have the same connection to people or place. Street-based public transport makes getting about easier and better connects you to place. You can more easily orient yourself since you always can see where you are in relation to people and activities, the things and places you know and use.

With street-based transport, there is also a particular dynamic of getting off at an earlier stop or going on to the next stop when required, which also increases familiarity with the assets of the neighborhood.

01./02. Berne, Switzerland. Eye-level mobility—tram and bus—makes for a personal touch—just ask the driver.

03./04.Bogotá, Colombia and Strasbourg, France. Travelling at eye-level along the street helps relate you to neighborhood life by seeing people going about their business; helps you orient yourself as you see places; and connects you to nature, as you are in the light, seeing the trees and the weather.

01.

02.

03.

04.

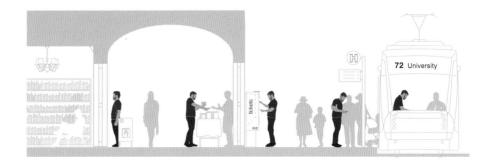

The Sidewalk as a Platform

Buses and trams are easily accessible when the sidewalk is the platform. It is easy to get on and off the bus or tram when it is only one step away. This simplicity ensures that people with a diverse range of needs have easy access to transportation. With low-floored vehicles, trams and buses can better deal with everyday urban equipment such as strollers and walkers, luggage and shopping bags.

There is also greater freedom and the possibility for spontaneity when public transport is accessed straight from the sidewalk. While walking, you might notice the bus coming and decide to hop on at the last minute to save a bit of time, energy, or get out of the rain. The sidewalk as platform allows you to be close to other people or keep your distance, to step into a patch of sunshine a few meters away, to sit on a bench, to grab a coffee or buy a newspaper, or run into the shop next door to get something you need. This arrangement affords you the opportunity to use every second until the last moment when you have to board because the bus or tram is only one step away. This simplicity offers you more options and grants you the opportunity to make efficient use of your time, making the whole business of getting about much more convenient.

01. **Hamburg, Germany.** The bus stop is part of the life of the street, literally a couple of meters from the restaurant. Note also the big open window of the restaurant making this street relationship even softer.

02. **Tokyo, Japan.** Just one small step—getting on and off the bus on the street—is convenient for people with mobility challenges, and the street itself is a safe and pleasant place to wait.

01.

02.

There is a simple logic that comes with sidewalk transport stops. You can see the bus moving along the street in either direction and instinctively understand how the route works and where you get on and off. There is the opportunity to intuitively work out when the next bus is due based on the number of people standing and waiting, which might be more accurate than the official information provided by printed timetables or on apps.

Rather than placing the transport hub inside a separate building or in an underground station, access to public transport can sit comfortably in the street environment. This keeps different modes of traffic at close proximity, and allows for a fluid shift between the modes. It means that transport options are visible, understandable, easy to navigate, connected to the surroundings, feel safer, and allow you to use your time efficiently.

Most of the street-based modes of public transport (trams, buses, minibuses) can potentially utilize the same stops and routes, which makes for an efficient, seamless, and highly adaptable system. The various forms of transport can provide different solutions for a diverse population with different needs.

01./02. **Bordeaux, France and Melbourne, Australia.** The sidewalk as a platform, the street as a station. Public transit immediately accessible and part of the life of the street.

03. **Vienna, Austria.** The ease of stepping on and off buses and trams directly from the sidewalk.

04./05. **Bordeaux, France.** The ease of stepping on and off buses and trams directly from the sidewalk.

01.

02.

03.

04.

05.

Public Transport as Part of the City:
Transport Hub, Berne, Switzerland

The covered public-transport interchange in Berne, Switzerland is a hub for buses and trams located directly outside a large department store and a church in the central business district. The transport hub is a continuation of the public realm, with no spatial or surface differentiation.

This situation makes the transport service very accessible and extremely convenient. Literally a few steps and a few seconds from a shopping trip or a church service, a dentist's appointment or a visit to the bank, you can be on a tram. This very simple solution gives access to different modes of transport, all under a distinct glazed roof, which also gives weather protection without shutting out daylight or views to the surroundings.

The open quality of the hub gives a feeling of security because there is high visibility. There are others out on the street, those in nearby shops, as well as people in apartments and offices looking onto the street. Additionally, the ease of access means it is also easy to exit in the case of danger.

One-Way versus Two-Way Streets

One-way streets became popular in the 1970s when they were thought to be a simple way to increase capacity and flow for vehicular traffic in urban areas. In reality, they can complicate mobility. One-way streets tend to prioritize thru traffic, which has literally no business in the neighborhood.

The driving culture of one-way streets, frequently with higher speeds, does not coexist well with other forms of mobility. For example, the faster flow of traffic going in one direction can make it harder for a pedestrian to cross the street. It is also challenging as a cyclist, and even if contraflow cycling is allowed, it can be particularly intimidating. Even for drivers, navigating a one-way system makes for more complicated driving as intuitive way-finding is lost, and longer distances must be travelled, which in turn creates more traffic, more noise, and more pollution. A report in 2010 found that two-way streets reduced total distance traveled by 8-16% because they offered more route choices and resulted in less unnecessary circling.[17]

In a one-way system, bus routes cannot run on the same street in different directions, meaning the instinctive understanding of the public transport system is lost. Your bus stop is not on the other side of the street where you got off, but on some other street, somewhere else.

Two-way streets can calm traffic, which often results in greater activation, neighborhood rejuvenation, and even higher property values. It has also been observed that the slower car traffic has a positive effect on the local economy as drivers discover businesses in the neighborhood.

01. The one-way street encourages faster driving while making wayfinding less logical. It's harder for pedestrians to cross and more daunting for cyclists. For public-transport users, it makes for a less understandable system as their bus home is on another street.

02. Apart from the convenience to car drivers for more logical wayfinding, the two-way street offers a better balance between different street users. The two-way street can be easier to cross for pedestrians, safer for cyclists (especially when there are no bicycle lanes), and easier for public-transport users to find their bus home.

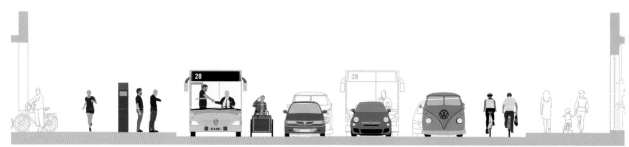

01.

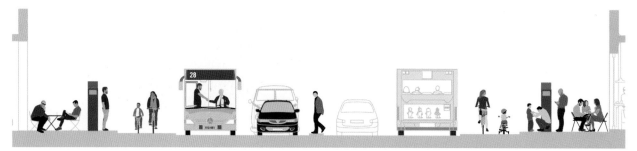

02.

From One-Way Back to Two-Way Streets:
Perth, Australia

Before

After

Perth, Australia, has been converting many of its main streets from one-way back to two-way as part of a bigger vision to create a more vibrant and pedestrian-friendly city. After a successful trial of changing one-way traffic to two-way traffic on William Street, one of the two main streets in the central business district, the city is changing main streets to two-way traffic throughout the city.

The changes also include improvements to the public realm with wider sidewalks, street furniture, and trees, improved pedestrian crossings, as well as road engineering changes such as tighter turning geometry for motorized vehicles.

The city has introduced the program with a high level of public consultation and presented the arguments for change in an accessible and communicative way.

" When you have a return to two-way traffic flow in any street, the traffic tends to slow down because there is that combination of traffic going in both directions."

Perth Lord Mayor Lisa Scaffidi[18]

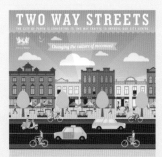

Leaflet issued by the City of Perth communcating changes.

Transport Corridor: Design Development Overlay

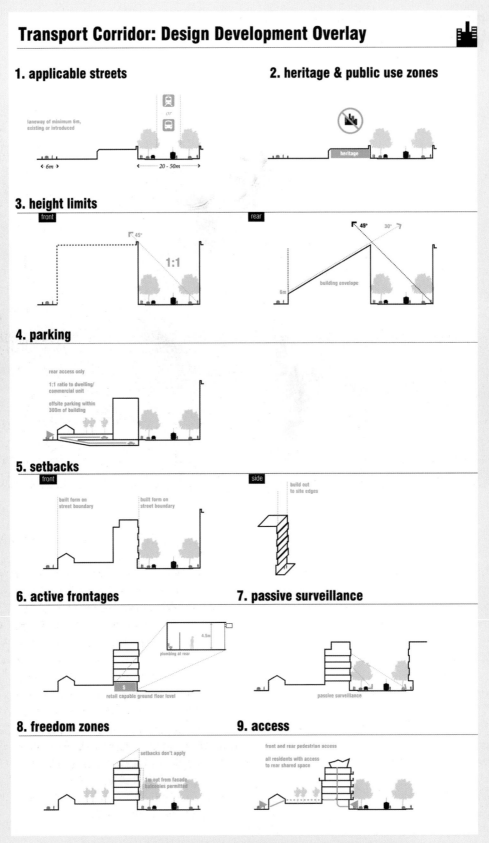

1. applicable streets

laneway of minimum 6m,
existing or introduced

6m

20 - 50m

2. heritage & public use zones

heritage

3. height limits

front

45°

1:1

rear

45°   30°

6m   building envelope

4. parking

rear access only

1:1 ratio to dwelling/
commercial unit

offsite parking within
300m of building

5. setbacks

front

built form on
street boundary

built form on
street boundary

side

build out
to site edges

6. active frontages

4.5m

plumbing at rear

$

retail capable ground floor level

7. passive surveillance

passive surveillance

8. freedom zones

setbacks don't apply

1m out from facade
balconies permitted

9. access

front and rear pedestrian access

all residents with access
to rear shared space

Planning requirements explained on one piece of paper, with simple diagrams.
Illustration by: Steve Thorn, Ralph Webster, Simon Goddard, City of Melbourne.

Densifying Around Existing Infrastructure:
"Linear Barcelona," Melbourne, Australia

Building on What is There

"We have reached an interesting time when the drivers of sustainable cities are the same as the drivers of livable cities, namely, mixed use, connectivity, high-quality public realm, local character, and adaptability. When these characteristics come together as they do in Barcelona, they provide an alchemy of sustainability, social benefit, and economic vitality. These cities reduce their need for car travel, reduce energy consumption and emissions, use local materials, support local businesses and create identifiable communities."

Rob Adams, *Transforming Australian Cities*, 2009[19]

Popularly referred to as "Linear Barcelona," *Transforming Australian Cities* is a report on the findings of a study by a team from the Melbourne City Council, led by Rob Adams, the director of city design for the City. The report makes the case for a strategic development model that would increase the density of the city over time, using the existing infrastructure and retaining the human scale of the neighborhoods. The approach accommodates population growth without outward expansion. The report shows how Melbourne can double in population while using only 7.5% of the developed land and leaving the remaining 92.5% untouched. Of the 7.5%, 3% is along road-based public transport routes; 3% is around rail stations; and 1.5% is in brownfield sites.[20]

01.   02.

The idea is simple: enable denser, mixed-use development along and around existing public transport, fast-tracking approvals of appropriate planning applications. This is enabled by Melbourne's extensive tram network, the largest in the world, and the city's suburban rail network.

What is appropriate is summed up by nine simple diagrams on one A4-sized piece of paper. Basically, Linear Barcelona allows independent apartment buildings no higher that six to eight stories with active ground floors (the typical European or Barcelona typology, hence the name) to be built fronting the identified main streets and around identified stations.

The study recognized that low- and medium-rise buildings require less embedded and operating energy as the stairs become an alternative to elevators when living at walk-up height and passive ventilation and cooling are possible with manually openable windows. Additionally, better microclimate is possible down on the ground level as there are no tall buildings to cause unpleasant wind turbulence.

By defining the height limits very clearly from the start, it is very easy for land value to be determined and realistic prices set. This helps to move the development along since developers are not waiting, perhaps greedily hoping for a bit more height.

The clear simple rules allow densification to take place plot by plot, property by property. This approach benefits small-scale developers, including the current site owners, local families and businesses, as well as smaller, local construction companies. These developers can independently develop their property in their own way, with their own particular style and taste. This makes for a pluralistic approach with many different interpretations, economic models, and specific architectural solutions. More projects and smaller projects make for a broader economic base, employ more diverse architects, and, hopefully, accommodate a diverse group of occupants.

Neighboring Areas

The human scale with walk-up-height buildings is also a neighboring scale. Development is at an appropriate scale for the surrounding, more suburban-style housing—much of it single story, so there is little or no overshadowing or loss of view. Densification at this scale can be advantageous to the smaller-scale neighbors, offering the opportunity to live in a detached, single-story house in a garden, in walking distance to the urban benefits of public transport, shops, services, and experiences.

The surrounding low-density areas balance the densification of the main thoroughfares. The idea is that as the local main streets are densified, the remaining low-rise, garden suburbs on either side are protected from development, traffic is calmed, and the area is greened. These green suburbs are areas of stability, energy self-sufficient with solar and wind power, and

03.

04.

with increased greening, in particular with increased tree canopy and zones of biodiversity, improving habitat for flora and fauna. Water-sensitive design, including harvesting rainwater and wastewater, as well as local sewer mining, reduce the burden on the existing infrastructure. Overall, these ecological hinterlands reduce heat-island effect and help clean the air, effectively becoming green lungs for the city.

Employing Existing Infrastructure

There are clear advantages to using existing infrastructure, both in terms of economic and environmental savings. Street infrastructure and utilities such as water, electricity, and telecommunications are already in place. The social and commercial infrastructure of shops and services are already in place. Greater patronage of the existing public transport can mean investment in better and more-frequent service. More customers can mean higher turnover for shops, with fresher products and a greater range of goods. For the city, it can mean a more concentrated population paying taxes to fund the services that everyone uses. In this way, this kind of densification can potentially benefit all.

Multiple Juxtapositions

Unlike larger-scale new developments, Linear Barcelona creates a natural condition of coexistence between old and new. The numerous individual projects mean that there are multiple juxtapositions, making for an urban dynamic with old and new buildings side by side, the

renovated and the dilapidated alongside each other, low rents next to expensive ones, meaning start-ups and pop-ups can be located alongside chainstores and established businesses. There is mutual benefit of this diversity, a kind of socio-economic ecology, as people are exposed to different experiences and people.

The Upgraded Street as a Public Space

At the same time, the new development can generate revenue to invest in improving the streetscape: higher quality paving to make for better pedestrian conditions and more street trees and water-sensitive planting, traffic calming, better cycling paths, and improved trams stops. Better detailing and materials, furniture, and landscaping can, in turn, increase the use of the streets by turning them into public spaces, where stopping, sitting, and spending time can be as important as moving about.

01. Typical existing conditions with low buildings fronting main suburban streets.

02./03. New mixed-use infill, Prahran.

04. Upgraded streetscape with new public seating, Prahran.

Time

A particularly interesting aspect of Linear Barcelona is that of time. The approach recognizes the value of speeding up the process of development by making it easier to plan and build. The model also recognizes the benefits of development occurring incrementally over time, in tune with the life of the people living there.

In the short term, Linear Barcelona makes it easier to get started. By clearly defining the limits, there is a sense of assurance that a better deal cannot be had and the landowner or developer might as well get on with it. These limits also assure neighbors that they will be protected from piecemeal or haphazard development outside of the defined zones, therefore eliminating the need to oppose or fight planning applications. Thanks to the simple and straightforward single page of rules, the developer can very clearly understand what is possible. The fast-tracking of projects through the planning system that fulfills these requirements means they can get started faster.

Unlike megaprojects with only new buildings, which require precise timing and create huge disruption, Linear Barcelona happens piece by piece, over years, and the community around continues to function more or less normally all the time, adapting and accommodating the changes, the new population, and activities as they come. Each piece has its own timetable, and whether it is finished earlier or later doesn't affect the whole. This aspect can be seen as a kind of time tolerance.

The genius of Linear Barcelona is that it builds on what is there, helping the city to work harder by doing more with existing resources. It adds to the city in a way that does not destroy or damage the existing, inherent qualities and allows the development to happen incrementally over time. In this higher density, new buildings coexist with the old ones. This is not just a question of accommodating different aesthetics or the visuals of architectural scale; this about different kinds of activities and people coexisting, new and old, public and private, side by side on the same street.

The *Transforming Australian Cities* study has a human touch, talking about people per hectare rather than building densities. It recognizes the human dimension, developing in smaller, incremental steps so that people can experience the benefits as they come, delivering not only buildings at a human scale but also change at a human pace.

Although some of the inspiration may have come from Barcelona, throughout the inner suburbs of Melbourne a new architecture is appearing, an urban vernacular, totally unique and belonging to its place.

This kind of development model is relevant for many other parts of the world, demonstrating that high density is possible without high rise, and that increased density can offer better quality of life for more people.

Melbourne's new urban vernacular architecture

The "Linear Barcelona" Model

Existing situation with low-density streets served by quality public transport.

In the short to medium terms, streets can be upgraded with trees, bike lanes, and furniture, and the first new buildings can be constructed alongside the old. New uses can be found for the existing buildings.

In the medium to long terms, the building stock can be replaced, densified, and diversified at a pace where local businesses and residents can be part of the journey. With increased population, public transport can be more frequent.

Diversity of Streets

It doesn't have to be a pedestrian-only street to be a people street. In fact, a street that accommodates different modes of transport can be even livelier when citizens meet as neighbors in traffic.

Thoughtful design can help streets to perform better in how they balance the distribution of different modes of traffic in space. The street space can also be designed, in time, to prioritize different users and allow different activities at different times of the day, week, or year.

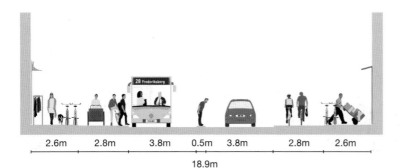

| 2.6m | 2.8m | 3.8m | 0.5m | 3.8m | 2.8m | 2.6m |

18.9m

Vesterbrogade, Copenhagen, Denmark.
The busy thoroughfare accommodates a great diversity of users, with cycle lanes in each direction and a thin median down the middle. The median is almost flat to make passing possible for vehicles on the one-and-a-half-lane wide traffic lane.

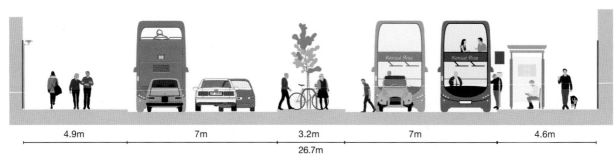

| 4.9m | 7m | 3.2m | 7m | 4.6m |

26.7m

Kensington High Street, London, England.
The street has been reorganized with a wide median strip for cycle parking, which makes it easier to cross the street and gives a signal about how to use the street—calming traffic. Previously, the street had barriers between pavement and traffic lanes. Since the change, there have been fewer accidents.[21]

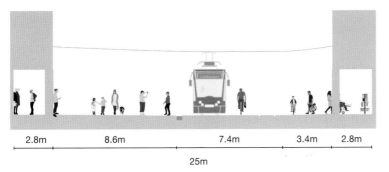

| 2.8m | 8.6m | 7.4m | 3.4m | 2.8m |

25m

Kaiser-Joseph-Straße, Central Freiburg, Germany.
The tram runs through the pedestrian street, as do main cycle routes. The merging of trams, cycles, and pedestrians requires a constant negotation between the different users.

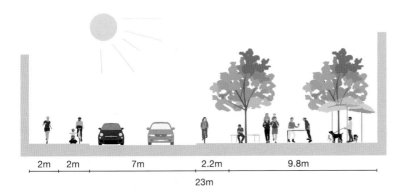

| 2m | 2m | 7m | 2.2m | 9.8m |

23m

Vester Voldgade, Copenhagen, Denmark.
An extra-wide pavement on the sunny side of the street invites people to stop, stay and enjoy the space, and take advantage of the pleasant microclimate.

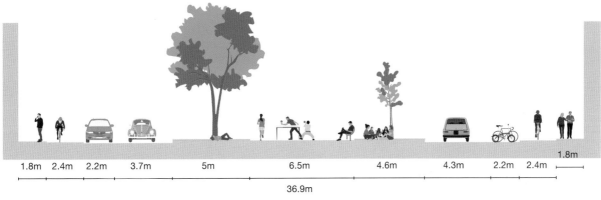

| 1.8m | 2.4m | 2.2m | 3.7m | 5m | 6.5m | 4.6m | 4.3m | 2.2m | 2.4m | 1.8m |

36.9m

Sønder Boulevard, Copenhagen, Denmark.
The park strip down the middle has been turned into a rambla-style linear park with greenery and a range of outdoor spaces for active and passive recreation.

0.7m   3.1m   0.7m
4.5m

A neighborhood street in Daikanyama, Tokyo, Japan.
A single asphalt surface with no sidewalks (apart from an occasional painted line) makes for a "traffic ballet" of intuitive negotiation between pedestrians, bikes, and motorized vehicles.

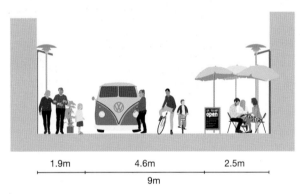

1.9m   4.6m   2.5m
9m

Strædet, Copenhagen, Denmark.
A pedestrian-priority street accommodates vehicle traffic and bicycles, but on the terms of the leisurely pedestrian.

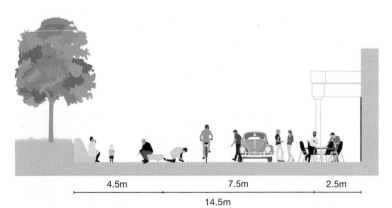

4.5m   7.5m   2.5m
14.5m

New Road, Brighton, England.
The UK's first shared space that gives pedestrians priority but also access to cycles, cars, and buses as long as they move through carefully. Photo: Shaw & Shaw

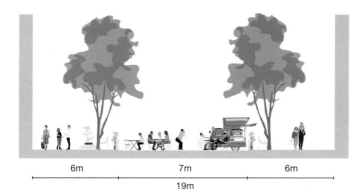

6m   7m   6m

19m

In the middle of the day

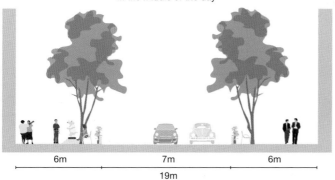

6m   7m   6m

19m

Mornings and evenings

Naka-Dori Street, Tokyo, Japan.
Naka-Dori Street has been softened with wider
pavements, street trees, benches, and artwork,
changing the character from finance district to
people place. The street is closed for a few hours in
the middle of lunchtime to give more space to the
thousands of office workers who work in the area.

3m   4m   3m

10m

One way in the morning

3m   4m   3m

10m

The other way in the afternoon

10m

Pedestrian street at lunchtime and holidays

Kagurazaka Dori, Tokyo, Japan.
In the lively Kagurazaka neighbourhood, the local
main street goes one way during the morning. It
is closed for an hour at lunchtime, and the traffic
goes in the other direction in the afternoon. The
street is also closed on holidays.

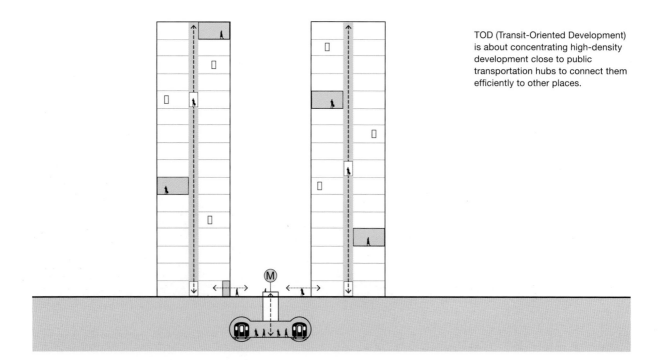

TOD (Transit-Oriented Development) is about concentrating high-density development close to public transportation hubs to connect them efficiently to other places.

Every moment spent moving between buildings presents an opportunity to connect people with place, with planet, and with other people. We should consider the overlapping and integrated experiences of mobility, part of what is ideally a seamless journey as you change modes of transportation: how you go from your apartment to the street, dropping into in a shop on the way; how you cross the street while interacting with other forms of traffic; how and where you park your bike; how you get to the bike lane from the sidewalk; where and how you wait for the bus; how you get on a tram; and then how you experience the neighborhood as you move about.

Therefore, urban mobility requires a holistic approach, accommodating a wide range of mobility options in the same space. At the same time, it is about considering how the smallest and shortest trips connect and feed into the larger and longer ones. Accommodating a diversity of mobility means making more options available, making it easier to get about in different circumstances and spontaneously change plans, and making hybrid or multi-modal trips possible.

We need to recognize the diversity of people who are trying to get about and their different needs and paces. We need to find ways to allow all of this difference to be accommodated and coexist in such a way that not only is active mobility prioritized but, ideally, the business of everyday getting about does more than get you from A to B. The time spent in between buildings in active mobility exposes people to other people in everyday encounters, simply seeing other people and noting how they behave, sitting next to strangers on the bus, overhearing conversations about unfamiliar topics, seeing the same people again and again, nodding to say hello and slowly developing broader acquaintances. These countless experiences and unexpected social opportunities, the frequent exposure to difference, the serendipitous

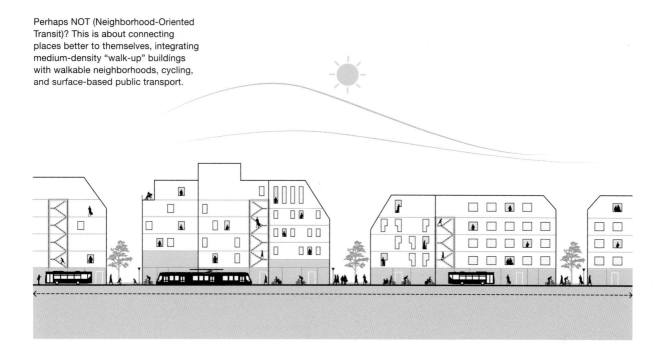

Perhaps NOT (Neighborhood-Oriented Transit)? This is about connecting places better to themselves, integrating medium-density "walk-up" buildings with walkable neighborhoods, cycling, and surface-based public transport.

and spontaneous, can make daily life more interesting. More importantly, the experiences can help build understanding and tolerance between different people and contribute to a more cohesive society.

In a similar way, active mobility exposes people to the forces of nature and the changing seasons every day. Spending more time outdoors, apart from the obvious health benefits, increases people's proficiency in reading the weather, learning from others, seeing how they dress and behave, and can help us better live the weather we have.

Much lauded Transit-Oriented Development projects use efficient engineering to connect higher-density, built-up areas to mass transit. In this way, they connect people efficiently with other places. However, I think the real challenge of mobility is as much about better connecting people to the place where they are. Rather than Transit-Oriented Development, we need Neighborhood-Oriented Transit.

Perhaps, ultimately, it all comes down to the basics of health and well-being—fresh air, exercise, and meeting people. Loneliness and obesity are epidemics. It is recommended to get at least 10,000 steps every day. Every daily trip offers the opportunity to walk more, stay more, do more outside, and spend more time with other people.

Mobility is about getting about, getting on with each other, and getting on with our lives.

The longest journey begins where you are.

Lao Tzu[22]

Layering Life

As we strive for sustainability and resilience in urban environments, is it possible to take inspiration from natural environments? In nature, there are systems that accommodate density and diversity in sustainable ways and have proven to be resilient.

A forest is much more than a big group of trees. It is a complex, symbiotic system that sustains the life of a wide range of species in different scales and situations. The forest offers habitat for a wide range of lifeforms—plants and micro-organisms, animals and birds. Forests are some of the most biologically rich ecosystems on the planet.

A characteristic of the forest is a distinct horizontal system of layering life. The life around the ground is different from the life in the branches, which is different from the life in the tree tops. There are different physical realities— dark places connected to the earth, light spaces connected to the sky, more protected places and those that are more exposed, and everything in between. The layering of these different micro-environments enables different forms of life to exist and even thrive in the same place.

Different species of trees may grow next to each other. Each tree creates its own environment and microclimate. The space between trees creates a unique environment, a product of both. In this way, the whole is greater than the sum of the parts.

What we know from the forest is that diversity is the key to sustainability. When the forest is attacked by fire, storm, or pests, it is resilient because the component parts can respond in different ways. Lightning can strike and a fire can start or bugs and disease can land, and even if a tree or two might be lost, or one species might suffer, the forest as a whole lives on. The forest demonstrates the potential for the co-location of different elements, creating a system in which the interrelationships let life flourish in the in-between.

Compared with the natural forest, a plantation of trees is very different. Here, there are no layers of different lifeforms. There is generally only one species. There is no difference created between trees, and the whole remains the same

Natural forest

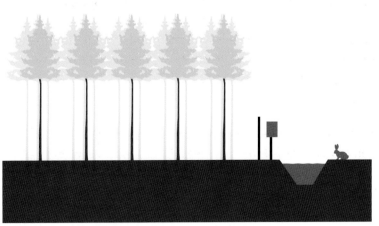

Plantation

as the sum of its parts. We know from the need for pesticides, the higher rate of destruction in storms, and the strict fire and flood precautions, that the planted woodland is more vulnerable than the natural forest.

It was while reading about the differences between natural forests and planted woodland that I was struck by the possible parallel in the built environment. Are there towns and cities that have the resilient characteristics of natural forests and others that are more like vulnerable plantations?

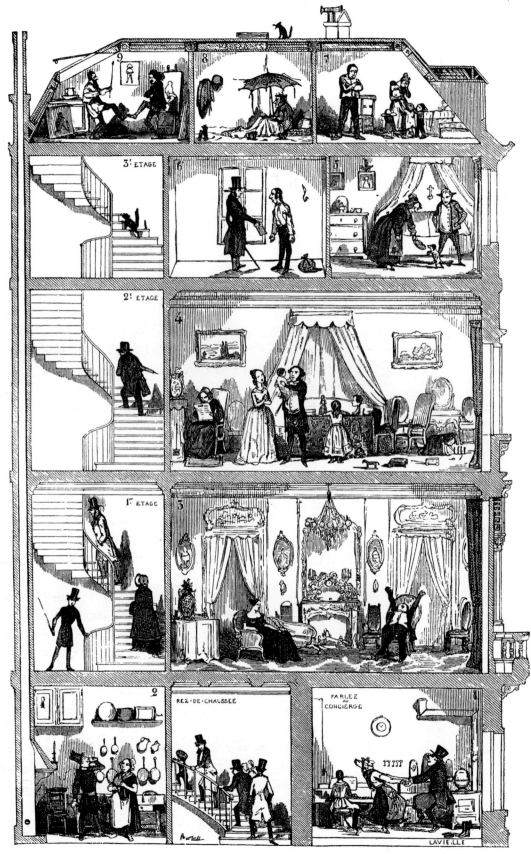

Cross-section of a Parisian house around 1850 showing the economic status of tenants varying by floors.
(Edmund Texier, Tableau de Paris, Paris, 1852)

The layers of different life seen in the traditional French apartment block are not unlike those in the natural forest. This drawing reveals the functional, social, and economic diversity that one building can accommodate.

The illustrator has tried to express the failings of society by exposing the innards of the city and the economic segregation of people. However, there may be another way of reading this illustration. What is truly significant is that all these different people share the same address. They all live under the same roof. The minute they step out of their apartment doors, they are neighbors; and the minute they step out of the building onto the street, they are part of the same community and have access to the assets of the city that might be found close by.

If this kind of diversity can be accommodated in one building, even more can be accommodated in one block, as the pattern is repeated. Therefore, it is possible for people with different abilities, needs, finances, and backgrounds, and at different points in their lives to all live as neighbors. It seems with most iterations of formal planning, even long before Modernism, there has been a tendency to try and make the human built environment in something tidier, which has almost always involved the separation of different people and uses. Unlike the people in the French drawing, today, people who are economically different from each other generally live many kilometers apart.

Is there a parallel between the natural forest and the traditional town or city? Just as the forest is not just a big group of trees, the city is not just a big group of buildings. In both cases, the total is greater than the sum of the parts. When it performs best, the city can also be a symbiotic and sustainable system for accommodating a great diversity of life.

Like the trees, the buildings can have distinct and different layers—the ground plane is the busiest and most concentrated, then there is the relative calm of the middle floors, and the special place at the top level, like the tree tops, where the buildings meet the sky. Are the segregated zones of Modernist planning, the social housing estates, the gated communities, the business parks, and the shopping malls the urban equivalent of the tree plantation?

Like life in the forest, urban life is in constant change. The local complexity provided by spatial layering and juxtaposition can allow a town or city to adapt and accommodate the ever-evolving changes of life.

Living with the Weather

in a Time of Climate Change

Green roof

Roof terrace

French wind

Recessed
balcony

Microclimatic enclosure

Loggia

Bay window

Biodiversity

Glazed
loggia

Deck

Arcade

As more and more people live in densifying built environments, the importance of spending time outdoors, encountering natural phenomena and learning to live closer to the seasonal cycles of the weather increases. The everyday experience of being connected to nature is a key factor in long-term health and well-being. Spending time outdoors also presents opportunities to meet other people and have shared encounters.

Everyone does not necessarily need to have their own garden, but they should have access to a range of outdoor spaces and experiences, from a window box to a roof terrace, from a balcony to a public park, from a sidewalk café to a tree-lined boulevard. These spaces can bring them closer to nature and help them live better with the weather.

Shutters

Balconies

Biodiversity

Street trees

Kayak café

Water features

Connecting to nature

River swimming

Learning to Live al Fresco

The Nordic countries, where people seem to spend a lot of time outdoors despite the generally harsher climate, are also some of the countries leading global efforts to address climate change.[23] It may be that people who are more in tune with their natural environment understand it better and value it more.

The images of Copenhageners cycling in the snow often shocks foreigners, especially those living in gentler climates. Just what motivates these biking Vikings? In fact, the city has a policy of clearing the snow from the bike lanes first, meaning that cycling is the first available means of transportation after a heavy snow. The weather becomes just a detail in a complex life equation where saving time is probably the most important factor.

Children in the Nordic countries also spend a considerable amount of time outdoors all the year round. From an early age, the culture of living outside regardless of the weather is established and often carried on into adult life. Cities need to be designed to encourage a culture of spending time outdoors in all seasons.

In Copenhagen, the Harbour Bath on Islands Brygge introduced sea-bathing to the citizens of the city. The public facility has helped establish new behaviors normally associated with holidays and vacationing at the beach. Swimming, games, picnics, eating ice cream, and sunbathing are all now part of everyday life in the city. The real change came from the decision to clean the polluted water in the harbor, including the contaminated river bed.

In Oslo, you can take the metro train, equipped with ski racks, from the center of the city straight to the ski slopes. In the summer, the same takes you to hiking trails. It is a huge bonus to have a convenient, direct connection on public transport from your daily urban routine to outdoor recreational activities.

Learning to live with the weather requires a sensitivity to change and a respect for nature. The spaces, form, and details of the soft city can help create opportunities to bring people closer to the forces of nature in small and simple ways as a part of their everyday life.

Copenhagen, Denmark.
Summer and Winter

01. After cleaning the water in the harbor, the Copenhagen Harbour Bath was established in the city center of Copenhagen in 2002—first as a temporary structure. It quickly became a very popular meeting place, and the structure was upgraded and made permanent. Later, a sauna was added to encourage year-round use.

02. Despite wind, rain, and occasional snow, 70% of Copenhageners continue to cycle to work in the winter.[24]

01.

02.

01.

02.

03.

04.

05.

06.

07.

01./02. A bathing station in Bogense, Denmark has a bathing jetty, sandy beach, ramp for wheelchairs, wooden boardwalk, and steps. The wooden buildings house changing rooms, toilets, and a sauna. On the rear of one building is a recessed bench that gently protects visitors from the cold northern winds.

03./04. Amager Beach Park, Copenhagen. An artificial beach designed to accommodate visitors and activities all year round.

05./06. Berne, Switzerland. Lightweight roof structures that extend the season. An old industrial building, which has been opened up, makes for an all-weather local community living room. A restaurant in a lightweight pavilion hanging over the riverside accentuates the connection to nature.

07. Paris, France. On the banks of the Seine, comfortable lounging furniture as part of the urban beach "Paris Plage."

Extending the Summer Season:
Copenhagen Café Culture

When tables and chairs were first introduced to the sidewalks of Copenhagen, the appropriate outdoor season was assumed to be short, not much longer than a couple of months. Denmark has a short summer compared to southern European cities where sidewalk cafés were more common. But the café owners and customers in Copenhagen discovered that sitting out is still quite enjoyable, even when the weather isn't perfect. Many cafés added blankets and umbrellas. Some have added heat lamps (less sustainably perhaps).

City records for outdoor café permits show an increase over time in the length of the outdoor-sitting season as well as the number of tables and chairs.

Copenhagen's outdoor café story is one of behavioral change with increased leisure time, and of learning to live with and make the most of the weather.

**Number of café chairs
in Copenhagen, Denmark**[25]

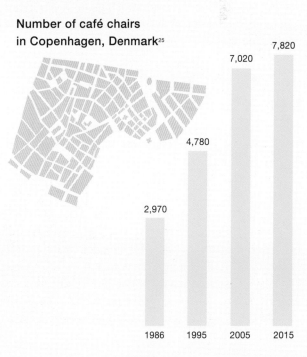

	2,970	4,780	7,020	7,820
	1986	1995	2005	2015

Bringing the Outside In:
Natural Light and Ventilation

Connecting to nature and the great outdoors starts inside the buildings where we spend most of our time. Having adequate, natural light and fresh air indoors has a dramatic effect on our health and well-being. There is no substitute for natural light. The dynamic qualities of natural light stimulate eye and brain function. Natural light improves workplace productivity and educational performance as well as healing and recovery in healthcare.[26]

Natural ventilation and daylighting are also two of the most obvious energy-saving features to consider when designing buildings. One-third of all electricity in the US is used on lighting, cooling, heating, and ventilation.

The convention in Modernist architecture is to get direct sunlight into buildings, but the designs can often end up being very one-dimensional. The method of measuring light is quantitative, based on direct sunlight penetration at certain times of the day—usually midday for dwellings. Designing for midday light is questionable, as this is usually the time of the day when people are not at home. Additionally, in some climates, an overcast sky is more normal than a sunny sky, and light filtered through clouds behaves completely differently than direct sunlight. Light requirements are complex and differ depending on time of day and the activities taking place inside. A diversity of light (and ventilation) conditions can potentially accommodate different activities in close proximity, which is desirable in a dense, multifunctional environment.

Lighting a space should not only be about the quantity of light, but also the quality of light. For example, natural light from more than one direction is very significant for the human experience inside a building. Christopher Alexander highlights this in *A Pattern Language*, with pattern number 159: "Light on Two Sides of Every Room." The quality of light and the human experience is dramatically different when this more complex light is present, influencing how you can read emotions and see facial expressions.[27]

The smaller dimensions of lower and thinner buildings increase the possibility of having natural light from two sides or even light from above. These dimensions give designers more options for abundant and high-quality light. Smaller buildings mean that circulation spaces like staircases, halls, bathrooms, closets, and corridors can have natural light and ventilation. A staircase with natural light and ventilation is more attractive to use, saves energy, and helps people to better connect between inside and outside. Lower buildings have proportionally more top floor, which

01. **Berne, Switzerland.** A simple casement window folds in to bring the outside inside.

02. **Berne, Switzerland.** A generous window in the staircase of this apartment building connects to life outside and makes taking the stairs a more pleasant option to the elevator. In the summer, the windows, combined with the "chimney" of the staicase, provide effective natural cooling.

03. **Tokyo, Japan.** A folding window opens up the café into a hybrid inside-outside space.

01.

02.

03.

allows more spaces to have light from above with skylights. A skylight can let in far more light than normal windows of the same glass area.

Vertical glazing is only effective up to six meters (approximately 20 feet) inside a building. Therefore, above a depth of 12 meters (approximately 39 feet), natural lighting is going to be limited. Smaller dimensions also allow natural light and ventilation into secondary spaces such as bathrooms, closets, and box rooms. This not only represents energy savings, but also the quality of life experienced in these practical spaces. Too often, we see taller and thicker buildings designed with windowless principal rooms like bedrooms and kitchens.

Natural ventilation is cheaper (ultimately free) than artificial ventilation such as air-conditioning, and saves unnecessary emissions and use of energy. An air-conditioned home in the US produces two tons of CO_2 per year. Five percent of all US electricity powers air-conditioning.[28] Natural ventilation is easier for the user to control and connects people better to the outside. Mechanical ventilation is expensive to install, maintain, and run. It aggravates asthma and allergies, and creates unpleasant noise. Additionally, many find the chilly feel of air-conditioned space unpleasant.

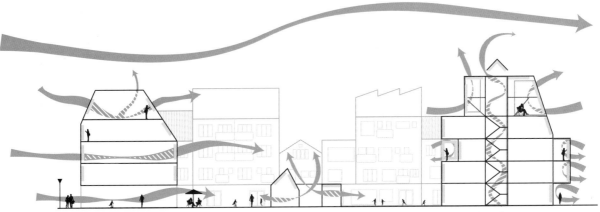

Smaller dimensions allow for more natural light and ventilation as well as create local microclimates.

There are some simple ways to achieve natural ventilation, all of which are easier to achieve in a smaller building. The best is cross-ventilation, with air entering on one side and leaving on the opposite side. A difference in temperature on opposite sides of the house creates air movement. Recesses and projections in the facade such as loggias, bay windows, and balconies, create shadows and a small but significant difference in temperature, which stimulates air movement.

Courtyards, patios, and light wells create microclimates distinct from the surroundings streets and squares, and the resulting temperature difference stimulates natural ventilation. Even details in the room layout of an apartment plan, such as the position of doors or having more than one door to a room, can stimulate better air movement.

01. **Malmö, Sweden.** Natural light from more than one side or from above greatly improves life indoors for homes, workplaces, and commercial spaces.

02. **Tokyo, Japan.**

03. **Sydney, Australia.**

01.

02.

03.

An Office Building Where You Can Open a Window: CH2, Melbourne, Australia

Photos: Diana Snape

At nine stories, CH2 in Melbourne is somewhat higher than a European 4-5 story block. However, it is far lower than many of the surrounding office towers. CH2 is a pilot project for the City of Melbourne's Zero Net Emissions by 2020 plan, designed with a wide range of sustainable features, from wind power to grey-water harvesting. Perhaps most impressive are the simple details such as shutters, windows that open, and accessible balconies on every floor.

What is also significant is the successful landing of a large workplace in the Central Business District that merges with its surroundings, with an active ground floor with shops and restaurants, and only a small lobby taking up the precious ground level, to make for a continuous streetscape.

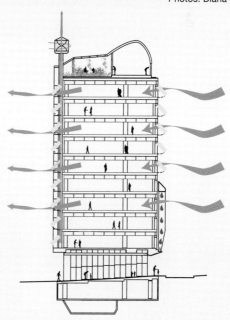

CH2 uses the forces of nature for natural cooling and ventilation.

Windows and Doors

Windows and doors are probably the most significant of all architectural elements. Beyond the pattern they make on a building's facade, and the air and natural light they bring into buildings, windows and doors can better connect inside and outside, sometimes blurring the two. Windows and doors can encourage us to spend time on the edge of buildings, improving our relationship with the outside. Therefore the most important aspect of windows is not only how they look, but what they can do.

There are many traditional and contemporary examples of window types that have the qualities that enhance the connection between the outside from indoors. Bay windows, oriels, and miradors, which project out from the facade of the building catch more complex light from different sides. These protruding windows also allow a better view of and connection to the outside spaces.

When layered—with storm doors, shutters, blinds and metal cages—doors and windows can do more, spontaneously adapting to the environmental and social requirements of the moment.

Tall vertical window openings, like a French window, offer a view that includes three significant components: the sky, the middle ground of urban surroundings with buildings and trees, and the ground plane where the people are. The sky and clouds inform you about the weather, while the ever-changing light tells you the time of day. The windows of the neighboring buildings light up at night, expressing human presence, connecting to the weather and the changing seasons while the leaves on the trees move in the wind. Seeing people moving about the floor of the city connects to everyday life.

French window—a vertical opening that affords a view of the sky, the surrounding trees and buildings, as well as people on the ground plane.

01. **Barcelona, Spain.** A windowsill bar allows restaurant guests to sit right on the street edge.

02. **London, England.** A mini bay window allows diners to sit in the street space in full daylight.

03. **Córdoba, Spain.** The cage over the window makes for a soft interface allowing the window to be left open and the sounds and smells of inside can be shared with the street. A rollerblind and plants add extra layers.

04. **Lucerne, Switzerland.** A wide opening in a restaurant with a generous windowsill invites people to sit, bringing a little of the street life indoors.

05. **Mexico City, Mexico.** Big windows allow the café to spill out onto the street while creating a microspace around the small table. Next door, the whole frontage of the tailors workshop opens up to the street.

06. **Tokyo, Japan.** Windows at treetop height make taking the stairs in this store a pleasure.

07. **Malmö, Sweden.** A window at eye level for neighborly conversation.

01.

02.

03.

04.

05.

06.

07.

An Intuitive and Responsive Filter Between Inside and Out: Barcelona's Shuttered Windows

01.

02.

The classic Barcelona window is a tall, vertical opening spanning from floor to ceiling, with a narrow balcony. The window is comprised of two basic elements: a pair of inner glass doors that either open inward or slide to the sides, and a pair of exterior shutters. When open, the inner glass doors take up no space in the room. The effect of opening them transforms the entire room into a virtual balcony, which affords the sublime feeling of living outside.

The fascinating thing about the Barcelona window is that it offers seemingly endless permutations of sheltering, shielding, and filtering the relationship between inside and outside.

On the outside, the two shutters fold in half to make smaller panels, and each of these smaller panels has two or three independent sets of louvres. These louvres

can be closed completely to make conventional solid shutters, or they can be angled upward, horizontally or downward. In this way, the louvred shutters make a highly complex and adaptable filter between inside and out, making it possible to adjust the acoustics, light, air, and visual relationship with the street.

The infinite combinations of the glass doors and shutters make it possible to maintain privacy while also bringing in light and ventilation. In this way, the window can be seen as an energy-saving device, providing both adjustable insulation and cooling without using any energy.

The Barcelona window is intuitive and easy to use. It responds immediately to the unique and precise circumstances and desires of the user.

03.

01./02. Two Barcelona corner
buildings offer very different
responses to climate. The
traditional one, with shuttered
windows, offers easy and endless permutations to the users
inside. The modern one is
inflexible and cannot respond
to the needs of individuals.

03. Six different positions of the
glass doors and shutters. The
simple combination of windows
and folding louvered shutters
offers limitless permutations
to filter light, air, and sound
between inside and out.

01.

02.

03.

05.

04.

Contemporary interpretations of the shutter are highly responsive, low-tech solutions filtering light, air, and noise into the urban environment.

01. Barcelona, Spain
02. Lyon, France
03. Basel, Switzerland
04. Freiburg, Germany
05. Melbourne, Australia

A Practical and Flexible Filter:
The Edinburgh Front Door

The traditional entrance door in Edinburgh, Scotland, is a combination of a heavy outside storm door and a lighter interior glass door. There is a vestibule or mudroom space created between the two that serves as a complex climatic filter, which can respond to the diverse daily needs of the users. Having a thermal buffer of two doors means there is better insulation and less heat loss when coming and going in cold weather.

The vestibule space can also accommodate outdoor clothing and equipment such as raincoats, rubber boots, and umbrellas typically used in rainy regions.

A fanlight above the storm door lets natural light into the hallway when the storm door is closed. The inner glass door may have patterned or opaque glass or even a curtain for privacy. The two doors, a lamp, and perhaps the curtain layer, provide different levels of connectivity to the street. Various combinations of openings by the door and curtains, and whether the light is on or off, act as a code for behavior on the street. Both storm door and glass door can be fully open or fully closed, or slightly ajar, and locked or unlocked, creating multiple combinations. These permutations can communicate the level of openness to sociability.

The expression of openness can also increase the perception of security, as a street, especially at night, can feel safer if lights are on and doors are open. In the same way, the lit vestibule can give the illusion of people being at home, potentially reducing the likelihood of burglary.

The Immediate Outside

The next step from the doors and windows includes the supports and spaces that allow you to spend time on the building edge, immediately outside. At ground level, this is about the space immediately around entrances, as well as useable hybrid spaces along the outside edge of the building such as porches, verandas, and arcades. On the upper floors, this is about the balconies, loggias, decks, and roof terraces.

One of the simplest details that encourages life to take place on the edge of the building is a roof projected over the edge zone. The classic example is the traditional Japanese house, with its overhanging eaves. This detail makes it possible to linger between just inside and just outside. With some kind of roof or overhang, you can spend time outdoors when it's raining or in unpredictable weather. You don't have to rush in or rush out. You can have a more relaxed relationship with the weather. It also allows you to leave stuff outside, such as furniture, equipment, or clothes, without them getting wet. This may sound banal in its simplicity, but this kind of convenience makes the living inside-outside, in tune with the weather, extremely easy.

The edge that exists right outside of a building at ground level, near or around an entrance door gives you a sliver of private space. This brings public and private life very close, and promotes encounters that can create community. Sometimes, there is no private edge at all, yet somehow, it can be inhabited or colonized with pioneering elements such as bravely placed potted plants or a temporary inhabitation, such as taking a chair outside while you need it.

01. **Tokyo, Japan.** 15-30 cm (approximately 6-12 inches) is enough to make a three-dimensional garden in this Tokyo edge zone. Note the sliding door and bamboo screen in addition to the bamboo roller blind and hanging plants that, when combined, make for a highly individualized and highly responsive filter between inside and out.

02. **Sluseholmen, Copenhagen, Denmark.** 90-150 cm (35-60 inches) gives room for a pram outside, or a table and chairs as well as planting. The discrete division creates a protected wall, and the change in surface marks the change from private to public.

01.

02.

10-15 cm (4-6 inches)

In as little as 10-15 cm (approximately 4-6 inches) along the edge of a building, there is space for a row of plant pots, an ashtray to be left out, or a place for a cat to perch undisturbed.

15-50 cm (6-20 inches)

With 15-50 cm (approximately 6-20 inches), there is room for bigger potted plants, a parked bike, and perhaps a narrow bench.

50-90 cm (20-35 inches)

At 50-90 cm (20-35 inches), there may be space for a little awning or small overhang. This offers protection from the elements and gives you a little buffer while coming and going. This edge zone might be enough that you leave the door ajar, and perhaps you leave a little chair outside.

90-150 cm (35-60 inches)

At 90-150 cm (35-60 inches), you can have a planting zone, a small table and a couple of chairs, space to park the pram or stroller sideways, or a couple of bikes.

150-180 cm (60-70 inches)

At 150-180 cm (60-70 inches), you may be able to have a table that you can sit fully around, or a chaise lounge. The more supports to comfort you can fit in, the more likely you are to spend time outdoors and socialize with your neighbors.

Simple Greening

The building edge is also a place where nature can flourish. Flora and fauna can thrive in an urban context when microclimates support and protect their ability to grow. Without getting involved in complicated vertical greening systems, simple measures and details like pots or planters, wires, trellises and simple metal or wooden frameworks can allow conventional buildings to support large amounts of greenery.

Spaces like balconies and outside stairs can be an ideal place for greenery. This adds to the green space of a city, which enhances our sensory experience. Instead of only seeing the gray of concrete and the sounds of people and traffic, we see green and follow the leaves as they change with the seasons, and hear the sounds of the leaves in the breeze. These elements of nature are important for our well-being. This modest green layer provides habitats for insects and birds and supports the local ecosystem. This living layer not only adds the beauty of nature to buildings, but it also helps to insulate and cool the building, purify city air, buffer noise, offer privacy, and reduce the heat-island effect.

Starting at the ground, the process of greening can begin with plantings along the outer edge of a building. In Lund, Sweden, the loosely laid cobblestones along the edge of sidewalks give residents direct access to the earth beneath, allowing planting of the street edge. This simple detail gives the residents the opportunity to cultivate plants right outside their homes, which gives something back to passersby on the street while creating a subtle buffer between the street and the building. This street-edge planting can be supported with small, metal protective frames or wires to facilitate growth up the facade of the building. The permeable surface of the loose cobbles also helps to slowly filter rainwater, so often the building-edge plants don't need to be watered. This spontaneous and modest planting along the street edge also acts as a reminder that there is fertile earth beneath the sidewalk.

The simplest of details can allow vegetation to flourish in the urban environment.

01./02. **Lund, Sweden.** By removing the loose-laid cobbles, residents can plant on the street edge.

03. **Freiburg, Germany.** Simple wires on a concrete facade allow a second skin of vegetation to grow.

04./05. **Paris, France.** Giant plant pots lining walk-around balconies.

06. **Stockholm, Sweden.** Ivy covering the front of an entire building.

07. **Freiburg, Germany.** Greenery on the metal framework of loggias.

01.

02.

03.

04.

05.

06.

07.

Porches, Verandas, and Arcades

Porches and verandas are very useful spaces, conveniently located just outside the door, with their own microclimates. The porch is an outdoor room, dimensioned for social activity. It is an intermediate space that acts as a vital buffer between the private realm of the home and the public realm of the street. Porches and verandas make relatively inexpensive extra rooms, which is especially significant for smaller dwellings. They create social situations and opportunities to engage with people on the street. There is something about the clarity of territories, which makes both the porch resident and the passerby feel very comfortable engaging with each other. The classic front porch in North America is an extremely important cultural phenomenon for enabling neighborly behavior.

The scaled-up and public version of the porch or the veranda is the arcade or colonnade. Apart from giving extra sidewalk space in higher-density urban environments, this simple architectural typology creates protected outdoor space for moving and staying. The arcade provides a protected space in which both formal and informal activities can take place. The arcade is equally useful for shade on hot, sunny days and rain and wind protection on stormy days. Most of all, the arcade is intuitive to use for promoting all kinds of sociability, finding the sweet spot of personal comfort, stepping in and out, leaning on the columns.

01. **Akaroa, New Zealand.** A simple roof over the sidewalk, in front of main street businesses, offers shade from the sun and shelter from the rain, allows goods to be displayed outside, and encourages passersby to linger.

02./03. **Sydney and Melbourne, Australia.** Supermarkets open up to make a soft inside-outside zone. Putting a café/bar function right at the front of the store, in this attractive space, invites people to linger rather than rush away, which is usually the case when grocery shopping.

04./05. **São Paolo, Brazil.** Two views of a café "porch" space, inside-out and outside-in. The glazed box of the terrace merges with the street tree and the sidewalk. A moveable bench makes a wall toward the sidewalk, but at the same time, also creates an ambigious soft edge with the small tables and the customers hanging over the edge.

01.

02.

03.

04.

05.

Balconies, Loggias, and Terraces

The convenience of the ground-floor hybrid spaces like porches and verandas is the relationship with indoor rooms that allows you to step straight out and step back in again. This convenience is also possible on upper floors with terraces, balconies, decks, loggias, and roof gardens. The immediacy and ease of access is vital to increase the likelihood of their use. Since there is much more security on upper floors, it is possible to leave possessions outside and leave doors and windows open (or at least unlocked). This is important for ventilation, convenient for pets and for children's play, and makes for more spontaneity and the feeling of freedom to move between inside and outside. The upstairs outdoor rooms also have greater privacy than their ground-floor counterparts and may invite more intimate dress codes and behaviors, such as sunbathing and hanging washing to dry.

Another important characteristic of successful balcony-type spaces is a degree of enclosure to increase privacy and get shelter from the wind. By being recessed into the volume of the building or protected with screens, a spatial complexity is introduced, enabling this kind of outside space to have a considerably longer useful season as well as a greater range of uses. Shutters, louvres, sliding doors and screens can help adapt such spaces to be more in tune with the exact needs of the user at different times.

However, it is also worthy of note that public or shared outdoor spaces on the upper floors are often considerably less useful, perhaps because of the lack of buffer between the public and the private, as well as an ambiguity of who the space belongs to.

01. **Freiburg, Germany.** Loggias with sliding, wooden shutters.

02. **Lyon, France.** An extra, habitable layer on building, with a glazed space with windows that both can slide as well as be opened with louvres.

03. **Malmö, Sweden.** Glazed balconies with folding, frameless glass panels allow a range of permutations from winter garden to fully open balcony.

04. **Malmö, Sweden.** A combination of bay windows and balconies creates multiple options for spending time on the building edge.

05./06. **Lyon, France.** Loggias with folding, louvred shutters offer multiple permutations for open and closed.

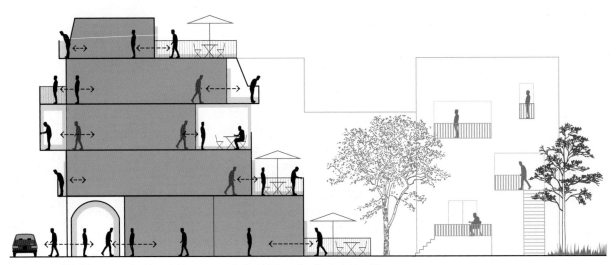

Hybrid spaces – Inside-outside spaces, all of which have "walk-straight-out" access.

01.

02.

03.

04.

05.

06.

Living with the Weather   171

Maximizing the Inside-Outside-Edge Experience: T-Site, Daikanyama, Tokyo, Japan

T-site is the flagship for the Tsutaya bookshop chain in the chic Daikanyama neighborhood of Tokyo. Conceived as a "library in the woods," this innovative retail establishment looks like a small village, with low-rise pavilion buildings set in a landscaped garden.

Rather than collecting everything inside in one interior space, there are nine pavilions. The bookshop takes up three separate pavilions, each with multiple entrances, where constant movement inside and outside is actively encouraged. Thanks to large windows, which are not blocked with shop fittings or shelves, there is plenty of natural light, accentuating the changing seasons. The bookshop boasts a café and a cocktail bar and is open until 2:00 am.

The other six pavilions house distinctly different activities: a specialist camera shop, an educational toy shop, an electric-bike showroom, a pet-service provider, a flexible gallery/showroom space for temporary events, and a bar/restaurant. The bar/restaurant pavilion is divided in smaller sections and has important covered inside-outside space to allow more time to be spent outdoors. The in-between spaces are rich in vegetation. There is a rock garden that invites play and a dog park that has as many spectators as users. The different uses invite people well beyond the usual bookshop customers.

Daikanyama T-site is much more than a bookshop. It is an outdoor destination, a mini-environment actively inviting life between buildings, encouraging people to spend more time outdoors whatever the weather, to encounter and experience difference, and to better connect to people, place, and planet.

Maximizing Vegetation in 3D:
Urbana Villor, Malmö, Sweden

Urbana Villor (Urban Villas) is a Baugemeinschaft (building cooperative). The aparment building has been transformed thanks to floor planters on the balconies. These offer a flexible surface with movable concrete slabs over a relatively deep, soil-filled bed. This allows for dense planting for foliage that might require deeper root systems. Combined with balcony railings and an external staircase, theses planters allow the building to support a veritable wall of green.

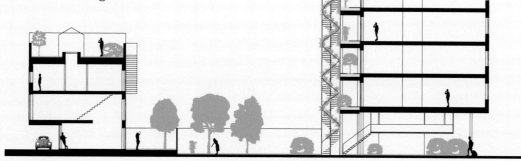

Maximizing Vegetation in 3D

Building Your Own Weather

Different regions of the world have different climates and weather patterns. These make for different relationships to the outside, with different cultures and behaviors. In the north of Europe, catching the sun and finding protection from prevailing winds are perhaps the most important considerations. In the south of Europe, it might be about finding shade. In climates with greater seasonal variation, a combination of spatial qualities might be desirable. The soft-city approach is about finding simple solutions to moderate the climate, and to reduce the extremes of the weather, so people can comfortably spend more time outdoors.

Protected from wind, and sometimes from the sun, spaces between buildings have their own microclimate, which is sometimes remarkably different from the surrounding climate. The enclosed space can make a place more inhabitable, allowing more activities to take place outdoors over longer time periods. This is similar to how a rock pool offers protection to allow more life, or how tiny plants thrive in the spaces between the cobbles. More things grow inside a walled garden than on an open plain. This notion of protection can be scaled up in the city, and the urban block can be seen as a big rock pool or a walled garden.

Although the urban courtyard is often smaller in area than the vast, open spaces between residential towers and slabs, it can be argued that the contained outdoor spaces within traditional urban blocks can be more valuable. These dense spaces can often be more biodynamically rich and diverse. The milder microclimate of the enclosed block enables increased use of the outside space, while spending more time outdoors supports sense of ownership and control over a space, as well increasing the likelihood of encounters with other people, which, in turn, promotes community. Additionally, the spatial clarity of the contained space makes for a clearer sense of identity and ownership, which can also result in it being used more. The open green spaces around many high-rise buildings, point and slab blocks that are often windswept and chilly, are less desirable places to spend time in.

At a slightly larger scale, the weather can be improved through a whole neighborhood with the layout or grouping of blocks. It is important to ensure that not only the private realms of the inner courtyards, but also the public spaces between the blocks, the streets and squares of the neighborhoods have a comfortable and pleasant microclimate.

There are lessons from old villages, towns, and cities, especially medieval ones, where asymmetrical layouts indicate that human comfort was prioritized over a

01. **Malmö, Sweden.** The sunny corner between medium-height buildings makes an attractive place to spend time outdoors, both on the private balconies and in the public space.

02. **Findhorn, Scotland.** Low rise, high density coastal cottages with pitched roofs create a more pleasant micro climate in the in-between spaces.

03. **Copenhagen, Denmark.** A suntrap in the corner of a courtyard.

04. **Lucerne, Switzerland.** Traditional, asymmetrical street layouts with narrow dimensions make for a better microclimate for walking and spending time outdoors.

05. **Breitenrain, Berne, Switzerland.** The wind-protected, sunny microclimate of the courtyard allows many options for spending time outdoors, both on balconies and loggias as well as on the ground, while at the same time allowing vegetation to flourish.

01.

02.

03.

04.

05.

neat pattern to the plan. Historically, many more aspects of life took place outdoors, and the microclimate of spaces outside was very important. Both in hot and cold climates, vernacular building favored smaller spaces and narrower streets. Streets in northern Europe, such as those in Stockholm's old town, have similar proportions to those found in Naples, Italy, in southern Europe, where one step can take you into the sunshine and one step can take you back into the shade. In a similar way, both hot and cold countries favored courtyard typologies. The common factors seems to be scale and enclosure, where smaller spaces and protected spaces offered a greater range of use.

In northern Europe, streets might be angled, with the wider space allowing for more sun exposure. The narrower part would protect the user from excess wind. Side streets might not be aligned with each other to stop the wind from howling through. What is fascinating when looking at old city plans, especially the ones we describe as "organic," is the response to climate and topography and the diversity of places created. Superficially messy, their apparent disorder is, in fact, a richer, more subtle order that responds to climate and the diverse needs of a society that spent more time outdoors.

Low- and medium-rise buildings protect the outdoor spaces from the wind and (depending on the local climate) the sun, making the spaces more habitable, as well as creating protected pedestrian routes thanks to a continuous edge. Also, lower buildings can be more easily ventilated naturally, resulting in health benefits for the people who use the building, energy savings for the building user or operator, and environmental benefits for the planet.

A sloping or pitched roof can be important in creating better microclimates. Sloping roofs have an aerodynamic shape that reduces or even eliminates turbulence in the spaces between the buildings. This makes outside spaces more pleasant because strong, gusty winds and colder, more-chilling winds are eliminated. This also makes it easier to have windows open for natural ventilation. A sloped roof allows the sun to warm and naturally light the street and courtyard spaces. From the ground, a sloping roof offers a bigger view of the sky, giving a vital sense of space and openness in the otherwise built-up environment. Perhaps most obviously, the sloping shape performs better than a flat roof, using gravity to let precipitation run off.

Smaller volumes such as outbuildings and small extensions help create even smaller climatic pockets. Working with smaller volumes also offers greater flexibility, allowing for very local adaptation to climatic requirements.

These simple aspects—enclosure, asymmetrical layout, aerodynamic roof shape and smaller built volumes—can drastically improve the microclimate of spaces between buildings, allowing more everyday life to happen outdoors.

Within the built environment, there are many examples of how urban form has created more-comfortable microclimates. The south-facing side of Lund Cathedral in Lund, Sweden, creates just such a pocket of microclimate. The sunny edge of the building and the wind protection from the church's buttresses means that the

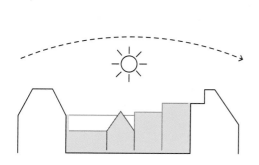

Enclosure

Enclosed spaces of the courtyards as well as consistent lower building heights create protection from winds, while lower heights enable the sun to penetrate.

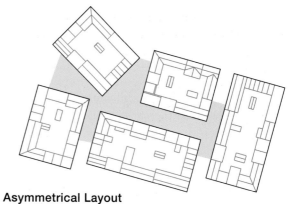

Asymmetrical Layout

An asymmetrical layout creates spatial opportunities for stopping winds and creates spaces with a pleasant microclimate. At the same time, the variation creates a more interesting experience.

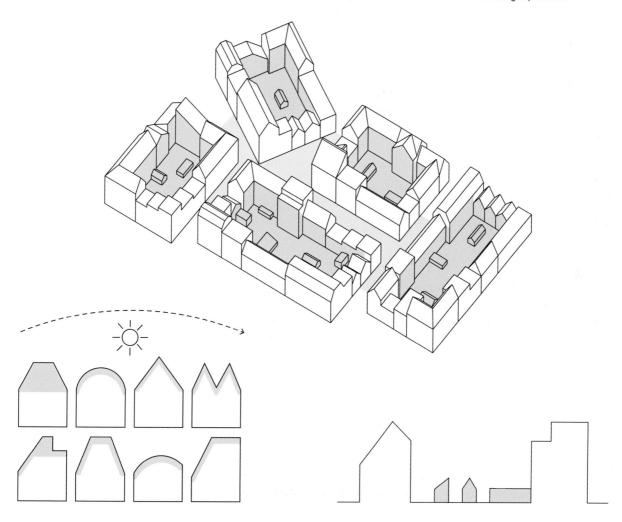

Sloping Roofs

The aerodynamic shape of sloping roofs allows the sun to access the street and courtyard as well as divert, slow, or stop winds.

Smaller Volumes

Outbuildings and smaller volumes help create good local microclimate.

heavy stone walls retain the heat and stay dry, and people can lean back and enjoy sitting outside on the long benches all year round.

Nearby, on the northeast corner of Stortorget, Lund's main square, people are able to sit outside even when there is snow on the ground because it is sheltered from the wind and catches the sun all afternoon. This corner is so popular that the city council has replaced the conventional benches with more comfortable reclined seating, a gesture to improve everyday, urban life. As people become more relaxed in the public space, and spend more time there, there are more opportunities to interact with strangers.

In Nyhavn, a harbor-side street in Copenhagen, the combination of the southwest facing waterfront and a wind-protected pocket has made for one of the most popular outdoor spaces in the city. Thoughtful organization allows commercial opportunity and public life to coexist. The street is organized into areas for walking and staying, commercial zones with tables and chairs under big umbrellas and occasionally outdoor heaters, and a strip of public space on the water's edge. Thanks to a diversity of staying and sitting opportunities, many different people can gather and spend time together in the same space, enjoying the natural aspects of evening sunshine on the water.

01. **Nyhavn, Copenhagen, Denmark.** The sunny side of Nyhavn has the best microclimatic conditions, used for both commercial seating under the parasols and informal seating along the water's edge.

02. **Lund Cathedral, Sweden.** Even in winter (note the long shadows), the south-facing edge of the cathedral makes for a pleasant place to sit outdoors.

03./04. **Lund Cathedral, Sweden.** The addition of small, movable stools/tables increases personal comfort and allows a greater range of staying activities to take place.

05./06. **Stortorget Lund, Sweden.** The northeast corner of the main square in Lund makes a sun trap and is a popular place to sit in summer and winter (note the snow on the ground).

01.

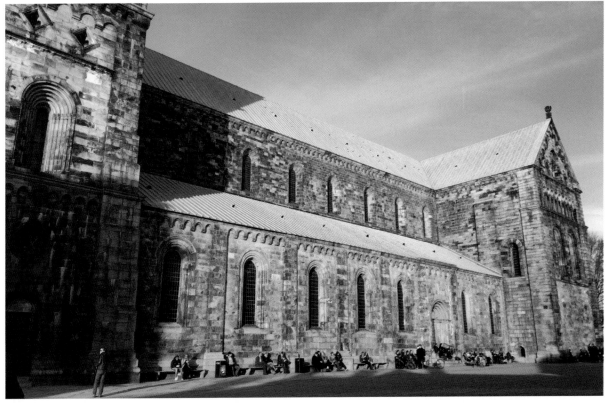
02.

03.

04.

05.

06.

Creating a Comfortable Microclimate in a New Development:
Bo01, Malmö, Sweden

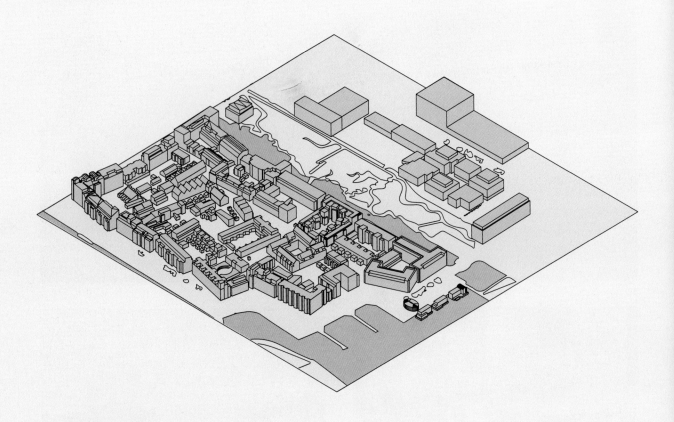

Build Density

Total area:	400 x 400 m /1,300 x 1,300 feet
Total floor area:	150,000 m²/1,615,000 sq. ft
Housing floor area (gross):	37,000 m²/398,000 sq. ft
Gross floor area ratio:	0.9
Site coverage ratio:	0.23

Ground Access

Build area with ground-floor access:	39%
Build area within ground-floor walking distance (4th floor or below):	83%

Bo01

As the name suggests, Bo01 was developed as a housing exhibtion in 2001. Sweden has a long tradition of housing exhibitions with the goal of showcasing new technological developments, experiments, lifestyle trends, and future visions.

Bo01 is a primarily residential development on an isolated and highly exposed brownfield site in Malmö's Western Harbour. The master plan architect, Klas Tham, created a neighborhood that accommodates both density and building diversity in an urban place with a village feel, offering a viable alternative to suburban life.

Bo01 has the spatial qualities found in medieval towns, with human dimensions and elements of surprise and charm. But the neighborhood is in no way a pastiche of the past. This neighborhood is totally contemporary in architectural style, in construction logic, and in materials and technologies used.

Klas Tham designed what might be described as a shaken grid. Based on a classic urban grid of square or rectangular blocks, Tham distorted the grid to create more complex spaces in between. The distortion is a response to the climate, shutting out the wind and creating welcoming and diverse public spaces that are oriented to catch the sun.

The rational rectangular shapes of the blocks reflect the building materials and components used in construction as well as the fittings and furniture that would be inside the finished buildings. The shaken grid maintains these rectangular shapes for the built form and ensures an economic rationale for construction and dwelling. The building industry is based on standardization, using the ninety-degree angle and rectangle as a base. It is expensive and time consuming to make irregular shapes in buildings; so this standardized approach was key to making the plan deliver more affordable buildings.

However, it is relatively easy and inexpensive to play with the geometry of in-between spaces. Planting beds, grass, gravel, asphalt, and even most paving can be easily adapted to irregular shapes. Unlike buildings, landscape angles with planting, grass, or paving don't need to be perfectly finished or water-tight. What some might dismiss as disorder, Tham describes as a richer order.

Plot-Based Urbanism

The already small blocks were subdivided into two or three plots each. Each plot was developed by a different developer with a different architect, meaning that there is a variety of housing types within the same block. The juxtaposition was initially unpopular with the developers, although there are stories of unusually high levels of competition between them when they were forced to perform side-by-side.

There is a mix of land uses, with a cluster of non-residential uses on the ground floor around the main corners. Additionally, the ground-floor spaces of the outer crusts of buildings have higher ceilings (minimum 3.5 m/12 feet) to allow for non-residential uses in the future. There is a range of dwelling types, with both houses and apartments, in different sizes and in distinctly different architectural styles. There is clear order of backs and fronts, with all buildings having front and

Zen view. The combination of the outer crust of buildings and the smaller volumes inside made for a climate protected inner world with only a glimpse of the sea.

back doors, creating more than one access option. The blocks are not all completely enclosed by buildings, but where there is no building, there is a wall or a gate to maintain the privacy of the residents' inner world.

All of the houses and most of the ground-floor apartments have private garden spaces in addition to the shared common gardens. The top floors have penthouse apartments and roof terraces with greenery in direct connection to inside spaces, as well as free-form, turret-like projections. In addition to the different private outdoors spaces, the blocks connect to different public spaces; the big seafront promenade to the west, the small squares with their water features, the local streets, and the small laneways. In this way, there is an exceptional spatial diversity in a very small area, allowing quite different activities to take place in very different atmospheres, all in extremely close proximity.

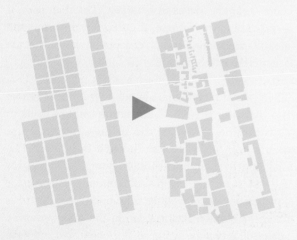

The Shaken Grid

The plan of Bo01 is a modified grid, creating variation and a good microclimate.

Movement and Behavior

The layout of Bo01 creates a clear hierarchy of spaces, with the public areas in more generous spaces on the outside edges and the smaller, more-intimate spaces in the interior. The relatively small blocks of around 50 x 50 meters (164 x 164 feet) make for a grid with an intensity of intersections, which encourages walking. The constantly changing urban scene provokes curiosity, making the explorer wonder what's round the next corner. The block layout also controls movement as not all openings are wide enough for cars, making for frequent pedestrian shortcuts.

Pedestrian behavior is different here thanks to the feeling of security that comes from having few cars traveling through. It is interesting to observe people walking in the middle of the street spaces rather than hugging the sides of the buildings—feeling the streets belong to them and clearly enjoying the spaces more.

Although cars are allowed to drive in most parts of Bo01, there are many other options that make more sense. Forty percent of residents walk or cycle to school and work, and 30% of all trips are by cycle. No one is more than 500 meters from a bus stop. Residents walk and cycle more and drive less than in the city center.

The pedestrian-friendly streets of Bo01 make a popular destination for local kindergartens.

01.

Attractive and Useful Outdoor Spaces

While the microclimate is a key aspect in making the outdoor spaces attractive and useful in this region and so close to the sea, the master plan also ensures a broad range of spatial experiences, with distinct spaces and outdoor rooms, from the most private and intimate to the most public.

Public space is a big part to the success of Bo01, from the major city destinations of the larger parks to the many small neighborhood squares. Bo01 is effectively framed by public space. To the west is the sea, and a waterfront promenade, Sundspromenad, and the green recreational park Daniaparken and to the east is the park, Ankarparken, with its seawater canal. These two significant public sides mean that there is no less-desirable backside. The two spaces have quite different microclimates. The waterfront has the big view, which attracts the crowds to see the evening sun. It also has the strong wind of the sea, which limits activity in some weather. The canal park has a calmer and more predictable climate, and is a quieter and more relaxed space. These two spaces complement each other, and their inherent differences create options for residents who can choose where they want to spend time and when.

01. Elevation of the Sundspromenad showing juxtaposition of different buildings to make up one street. Collage: Sotaro Miyatake

02.-04. A significant behavior is residents leaving their doors open and their personal effects spilling out onto the street, demonstrating a culture of spending more time outdoors, as well as a level of trust we would associate with an old, rural village and not a relatively new, urban development.

05. A pergola in one of the small public spaces.

02.

03.

A Green Neighborhood

At Bo01, the plan included a so-called green-space factor, which address the benefits of elements supporting biodiversity. In the same way as every plot had a different building architect, each also had a different landscape architect, ensuring a variety of solutions. The developers and their designers used a point-based system for each site, which allowed for a diverse range of solutions to interpret the green needs of the areas around their buildings. Points where awarded for large trees and bushes, green surfaces and plant beds, greenery on walls like creepers and climbing plants, green roofs such as sedum, water surfaces like ponds and other water features. There was a list of 35 wide-ranging environmental measures, at least 10 of which should be implemented in each residential courtyard.

Green points have been awarded for including a bird nesting box for every apartment and a bat box for every plot, leaving part of courtyard garden to grow wild; planting a garden containing fifty native wild flowers; green roofs; and systems to capture and resuse rainwater. The green-space factor is used when appropriate in the city of Malmö. Similar green-space factors have been used in German cities such as Berlin and Seattle in the US. More and more cities are considering green factors to meet the demands for greenery and biodiversity in a more dynamic way.

04.

05.

Pleasant Mcroclimate

Bo01 is on an extremely exposed site in the Öresund Straight. Although the location offers spectacular views and direct access to the water, it created a challenge in ensuring a pleasant and comfortable microclimate to allow inhabitants to spend as much time as possible outdoors.

In response, an outer crust of medium-rise (four-to-six story) buildings was built to effectively create a wall to protect the development from the wind. In the interior, the buildings are lower with one to three stories. The buildings either have pitched roofs or the top floors step back to deflect the wind and allow the sun deeper into the outdoors spaces. The blocks create courtyards with their own protected microclimate. There are occasional small breaks in the blocks enclosure to allow sun and light into the in-between spaces.

01.

In plan the blocks are skewed, narrowing in places to keep out the wind and widening to make sun traps of the public spaces. The blocks break down with smaller rectangular components to create staggered laneways and zigzag openings to ensure that the wind doesn't penetrate. This care for the microclimate was vital to encourage walking and spending time outdoors.

To investigate the actual microclimate effect of the layout in Bo01, Henning Larsen carried out a study of the microclimate. The study shows clearly that the attempts to stop the strong western winds and create shelter inside the neighborhood are working. On a March day with average temperatures around nine degrees Celsius (48 degrees Fahrenheit), many of the streets and spaces between the buildings will have comfortable experienced temperatures of 16-18 degrees Celsius (60-64 degrees Fahrenheit). In some places the experienced temperature is as high as 21 degrees Celsius (70 degrees Fahrenheit). The vast majority of the plan has higher temperatures than the actual temperature, despite the windy location toward the sea with dominant winds from the west-southwest.[29]

Below   8-10   10-16   16-18   18-21+

Micorclimate Analysis, Bo01, by Henning Larsen. The study shows how the layout creates protection from the dominant western winds, creating differences in experienced temperatures on a March day, ranging from 8 to 21 degrees Celsius (46 to 70 degrees Fahrenheit).[30]

Built-in Complexity

The plan makes for complexity within complexity. For example, one of the corner blocks is divided into four separate plots, each with its own developer and each a unique project by a different architect and landscape architect. The corner building has a café-restaurant on the ground floor. The middle building has an office and a salon on its ground floor. There are apartments with sea views on the western and northern sides (the outer crust) while on the inside, to the east and south, are terraced and semi-detached houses. The scale is from 1.5 to 6.5 stories, with an average of about 3.5 or 4 stories.

It is remarkable that the semi-detached house can be on the same block as an urban café terrace. The plan allows for very different spatial conditions to coexist in the same location. Another remarkable detail is the range of outdoor spaces one little house can have. The semi-detached house has its own private, walled garden and its own private roof terrace, as well as access to a large shared garden with a generous lawn shared with the other neighbors. In addition to these private and shared spaces, there is a small square with a water feature and a pergola just outside the front door, and access to a range of public spaces and the sea, all just minutes away on foot.

Bo01 as Game Changer

Bo01 has been a game-changer in neighborhood planning, creating a residential area that is a vibrant part of the city, where visitors and residents share many of the public spaces. In a region with relatively inexpensive suburban, detached housing and a strong culture of driving, it was a major breakthrough to attract former villa dwellers and families with children to a more urban context. Bo01 persuaded them that it is possible to have a high quality of life that is in close proximity to others and does not require driving a car.

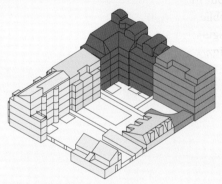

The block is divided into 4 separate plots, each a unique legal entity, with a different developer, architect, and landscape architect.

02.

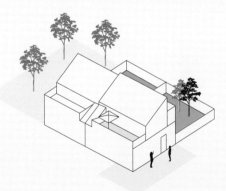

The semi-detached house is part of small housing association that includes the larger apartment building. The residents have a choice of outdoor experiences, with both a private roof terrace to the front and a private garden to the rear, a shared lawn as well as the small, public square just outside the front door.

01. The many protected sunny edges encourage people to spend more time outdoors.

02. Sea bathing is popular in the neighborhood, and it is a common sight to see residents walking about in their dressing gowns, which adds to the intimacy of the area.

Bringing Nature into the City

Biophilia is the affinity humans have to connect with nature. There are also many health benefits that come with encounters with nature. International research has demonstrated the healing benefits of seeing trees for hospital patients, and the Japanese practice of forest bathing is becoming well-known.

There may not always be natural landscape close by to connect with, so the experience of nature, or at least strong elements of nature, may need to be brought into the city. There are many ways to bring greenery and water back into the urban environment.

Although vegetation is probably the most important aspect of nature in improving the environment of urban places, the presence of water may be the most special. The strongest sensory experiences are associated with water, in particular running water, with sound, movement, and reflection.

01.

02.

01. **Mariatorget, Stockholm, Sweden.** At Mariatorget, a popular, centrally located park-square, the existing sounds of nature have been accentuated. The rustling of the leaves on the trees and the swooshing of the water in the fountains have been amplified via small loudspeakers, drowning out the noise of traffic.

02. **Basel, Switzerland.** As today's citizens become more comfortable with urban life, and as attitudes to using public space become more relaxed, old infrastructure, furniture, and equipment can be used in new ways. Here, the children of Basel use a historic fountain outside a church as a mini swimming pool.

Density and Diversity of Uses and Users:
Bryant Park, New York City

One example of nature in a very urban context, and therefore worthy of particular mention, is Bryant Park in New York City.

Inspired by William Whyte, one of the most significant design decisions was to insist on movable chairs, to empower the users, allowing them to sit wherever and in whatever orientation they wanted. Bryant Park was one of the first public parks in the US to have café-style chairs and tables for public use, without the obligation to buy and consume something. This allows you to bring your own picnic and creates synergy with surrounding businesses. Another key design decision was to lower the ground level of the park, making it nearly flush with surrounding sidewalks and stripping away hedges and fences to make the park visibly and physically fully accessible.

There is a range of different-sized spaces for individuals, couples and groups; busier or quieter corners; and a flexible range of events and happenings including open-air cinema, live sports broadcasts, seasonal shopping, winter ice-skating rink, an open-air reading room (a tradition dating back to 1935), petanque, table-tennis, board games, art classes, and a carousel.

Bryant Park is characterized by density and diversity, inviting a broad range of people to spend time outside doing a very broad range of activities from working at their laptops and reading, to doing yoga and line-dancing. The park offers a high level of service, including food and drink options, clean public toilets, and free internet.

A Small Water Feature with a Big Effect: Bächle, Freiburg, Germany

In Freiburg, small and shallow channels of water run through the streets of the medieval core, reinterpreting a historical system of small streams. These *Bächle* are 20-50 centimeters (8-20 inches) wide and 5-10 centimeters (2-4 inches) deep. The water channels have multiple functions: cooling and cleaning, acting as a separator between pedestrians and trams, or defining a zone for sitting and staying. They reflect a dancing light in the narrower, dark streets. Perhaps best of all, they turn the streets into a giant playground, offering children of all ages temptation and opportunities to sail small boats, paddle, and splash about.

This very small feature has significantly larger consequences, allowing the streets to do more by increasing the intensity of use. The Bächle help achieve the balance between recreation (staying, sitting, and playing) and function (multi-modal traffic corridors).

A Playful Place in Front of the Parliament:
Bundesplatz, Berne, Switzerland

The Bundesplatz is one of Berne's most intensively used spaces, with regular markets, demonstrations, and cultural events throughout the year. It has playful water jets that add an extra layer of life to the space, increasing the capacity and use of the square, making more of all the in-between time.

Making a playground right in front of the Houses of Parliament caused much debate over how appropriate it is for young children to run about barely clothed in front of the country's most important government building. In the end, it was recognized that the innocence of children playing safely in the middle of the city was the best reminder of the core values that the parliament represents. Although Berne has a river and many other water features, the simplicity and accessibility of the water jets changes a hard, formal space into a playful place for social and sensory experiences.

Street Trees

Planting street trees is one of the most significant things that can be done to improve an urban environment. Beyond their inherent beauty, street trees do many useful things that help improve the look, feel, and performance of urban spaces.

Trees change the climate of streets (and whole cities) by providing buildings and street surfaces with shade from the sun and protection from the wind. This makes it more pleasant to spend time outdoors on the sidewalk and easier to move about on foot and bicycle or wait for transit. In this way, trees have an important role in supporting active mobility.

More than a mere green surface, trees help reduce the heat-island effect, which blights many urban places, through shading, reflectance, evaporative cooling, and evapotranspiration. Trees act as privacy screens in densely built areas. They filter strong sunlight, reducing glare, and can act as light reflectors, throwing a dynamic "dancing" light into buildings. Trees provide a hugely significant sensory experience for people in streets with their sounds, smells, and movements. Their ever-changing appearance gives people an awareness of the seasons and the passing of time, and effectively turn streets into linear parks.

Trees absorb carbon dioxide. Since cities produce most of the carbon dioxide, it makes sense to place trees at the source of the problem and where people are most vulnerable. Trees are natural air filters, capturing dust and other particles from the air by trapping them on their leaves and in their bark, as well as absorbing unpleasant smells and pollutant gases such as ammonia, sulphur, and nitrogen oxides. This is particularly significant in relation to vehicle emissions.

01. **Sydney, Australia.** Street trees in a residential area create an intimate scale, improve walking conditions, and connect people to the changing seasons.

02. **Havana, Cuba.** Street trees form a canopy that creates an outdoor room and softens the climate for walking and staying.

01.

02.

Addressing Climate Change:
Urban Forest Strategy, Melbourne, Australia

Photo: David Hannah

The City of Melbourne has recognized the vital role that trees play in addressing health, removing pollution, and reducing the heat-island effect as well as simply shading the sidewalks. Planting an urban forest is part of their strategy to address the pressure that climate change, population growth, and urban heating put on the built fabric, services, and people of the city. "A healthy urban forest will play a critical role in maintaining the health and liveability of Melbourne."[31]

The concrete goals of Melbourne's Urban Forest Strategy include an increase of the tree canopy cover from 22 percent to 40 percent by 2040, and increased forest diversity. The goal is also to inform and consult, to make the trees even more relevant for the community.

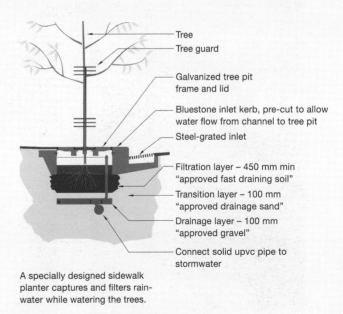

Tree
Tree guard
Galvanized tree pit frame and lid
Bluestone inlet kerb, pre-cut to allow water flow from channel to tree pit
Steel-grated inlet
Filtration layer – 450 mm min "approved fast draining soil"
Transition layer – 100 mm "approved drainage sand"
Drainage layer – 100 mm "approved gravel"
Connect solid upvc pipe to stormwater

A specially designed sidewalk planter captures and filters rainwater while watering the trees.

Connecting to the Nature That is There

Almost every town or city has some natural amenity, whether it's some kind of water, topography, or views. The way a place connects to its natural amenities and works to accentuate the best features, however modest, can have a significant effect on how much time people spend outdoors. Supports can be put in place to encourage people to spend time outside and encounter nature, and can also extend their comfort zone, making the experience feel easy, desirable, and pleasurable. This could include orienting new buildings to allow views of nature, uncovering a natural stream or river, planting street trees allowing microhabitats to bloom, or simply placing furniture outside of a café, allowing people to sit in the sun.

All of these encounters with nature, as grand as a view of mountains and as subtle as the sound of a birdsong, are significant and provide us with a strong awareness of the circle of life. Being aware of nature is the first step to understanding it, learning how to adapt to the environment, and living with it.

The simplest form of connecting people to nature is making what's already there easily accessible. In Freiburg, Germany, the Dreisam River runs just outside the medieval core. In the summer months, people sit on rocks in the river and enjoy its cooling effect and the shade from the trees on the riverbank. The rocks make for an informal sitting landscape, offering encounters with people as well as with nature. Even a small water surface of a few centimeters/inches deep, such as the stream that flows through the center of Kyoto, Japan, can have a strong presence.

The huge significance and value of water has been recognized in cities like Århus in Denmark and the South Korean capital Seoul, both of which have gone to considerable lengths to reopen rivers previously hidden under road infrastructure. The results of these efforts have radically changed the behavior of the people and dramatically increased the amount of time spent outside.

01. **Freiburg, Germany.** The Dreisam River runs just outside the city center, with natural elements for sitting.

02. **Kyoto, Japan.** A few centimeters/a couple of inches of water is enough to make for a strong sensory experience.

03. **Århus, Denmark.** The reopening of the river in Århus has created a new and very well-used recreation space in the city center.

04. **Seoul, South Korea.** The redis-covered river is an iconic pro-ject, distributing an exceptional sensory experience through the central city.

01.

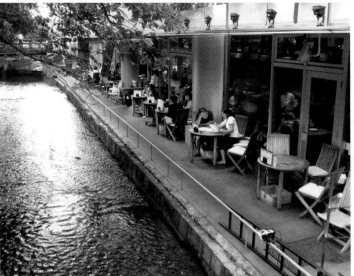

02.

03.

04.

An Outdoor Living Room for the Whole City:
Västra Hamnen, Malmö, Sweden

01.

The Swedish city of Malmö had historically turned its back to the sea, but with the redevelopment of the Western Harbour from industrial zone to residential neighborhood, the value of the waterfront was rediscovered. The flagship Bo01 housing exhibition, introduced the Sundspromenad, a pedestrian waterfront, giving the area a resort-like feel. The pedestrian waterfront is probably the most important public space in the city.

The main feature is a multifunctional stepped wall, which functions as a storm barrier, a wind break, a seating landscape, a playground, a stage, a catwalk, a sunbathing deck, and a viewing platform that marks and accentuates the spectacular view over the water toward the Öresund Bridge and Copenhagen.

Further along in the adjacent park, Daniaparken, enclosed, wind-protected areas afford a longer season of sitting outside and sunbathing while platforms, steps, and ladders into the sea make sea-bathing easier. The removal of dangerous rocks on the seabed has made diving possible, and the spectacular end of the promenade look-out point now doubles as a diving board.

Sundspromenad and Daniaparken attract visitors from the immediate neighborhood, the larger city, and even the surrounding region. Malmö has long stretches of beach, yet every day people of every age, ethnicity, and socio-economic background, come to the Sundspromenad, proving that an urban experience of nature can be just as attractive as a natural one.

02 .

03.

04.

05.

06.

07.

Accommodating many kinds of activities, passive and active, and many kinds of people in the same place at the same time, with many opportunities and invitations to spend more time and do more outdoors. Importantly, there are many practical, small details that allow people to get closer to the phenomena of nature, making it comfortable to sit in the sun or step in and out of the sea.

01. The stepped boardwalk becomes a small stage for tango dancing on spring evenings.
02. Swimming and sunbathing—note the windbreak walls.
03. Look-out point diving platform.
04 Water features offer entertaining play opportunities for children while adults relax.
05. Local children selling homemade juice to visitors.
06. All ages swimming and sunbathing.
07. Locals "eating out" in the evening.
08. Wind-protected outdoor room for enjoying the sunshine all year round.

08.

Making the Most of Infrastructure:
Taasinge Square, Climate Neighborhood, Copenhagen, Denmark

In recent years, Copenhagen has been hit by more frequent and more severe rainstorms, which have led to extreme flooding, causing extensive damage. In response to this new challenge, the City has developed a climate-adaptation plan, which calls for the creation of new soft landscaping in public places to absorb flooding.[32]

Spaces that previously had hard, impervious surfaces are being landscaped to accommodate flood water and allow slower run-off during and after rainstorms. Instead of investing in expensive underground infrastructure that is invisible to citizens and unused most of the time, the City has leveraged the investment in stormwater management to create greater value. The 2011 plan includes "Cloud Burst Projects" for more than 300

parks, streets, and squares to be implemented over the coming decades. The new landscapes improve the everyday quality of life for Copenhageners while increasing property values, increasing biodiversity, and reducing the heat-island effect.

One such new public space is Taasinge Square in Copenhagen's first climate-resilient neighborhood, part of the City's Climate Plan. The square that used to be covered in asphalt and parked cars has been transformed into a distinctive, green, and sustainable landmark. The park's response to stormwater is above-ground, and therefore visible to everyone. The space promotes understanding of climate change in an active social context. When it's not flooded, it's a great recreational landscape for everyone to enjoy.

Repurposing Infrastructure as Public Space:
Kizu River Waterfront Project, Osaka, Japan

The Japanese are accustomed to climatic disasters. Tsunamis, earthquakes, landslides, floods, and volcanic eruptions are all regular events. Japan has invested in hardware (infrastructure) and software (training) to ensure the safety of its citizens. High flood-defense walls protect cities like Osaka from the risk of flooding, but the walls disconnect citizens from their living waterfront. The scale of the walls eliminates any communication with the water, and the citizens lose their awareness of the sea, forgetting both their fear of and their delight in the water.

Ryoko Iwase's project from 2013-2017 repurposes the flood-defense wall, converting the hard, engineered infrastructure into public space, a terraced landscape with room for varied interpretation, inhabitation, and appropriation by the users. There is a continuous footpath along the water's edge to encourage people to walk by the water. There are big steps for sitting, inviting people to stay and watch the water. There is also a system of planters, which softens the concrete structure with vegetation. The citizens are invited to actively tend the greenery. By reimagining infrastructure as public space, people now have the opportunity to spend more time outdoors, connecting to the forces of nature both passively and actively.

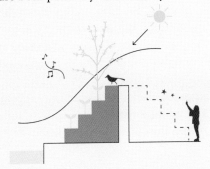

Making the Most of Nature:
River Swimming in Berne, Switzerland

01.

Imagine leaving your crowded office or your tiny city apartment, hot and sweaty on a summer's day, walking just a few hundred meters and then jumping straight into the cooling waters of a river. Swimming in the Aare River in Berne is an example of an activity that makes dense city life more enjoyable. It is the opportunity to connect, physically and mentally, to the natural environment in the middle of a city. The experience engages the senses: feeling your skin submerged in the water, putting your head underwater to hear the sounds of the stones on the river bed while hearing the splashing and voices of fellow swimmers and the sounds of birds and trees on the riverbank.

In these exceptional circumstances, there is opportunity to meet and interact with your neighbors and fellow citizens. Since the current carries people downriver, there is a ritual of getting in at the concrete steps or jumping off a footbridge, swimming with the flow, then getting out, walking back along the promenade to where you started, and then doing it all over again.

It might seem like an unlikely activity for the reserved citizens of the Swiss capital, but this natural wonder brings people from all kinds of backgrounds together in extremely relaxed circumstances. The bankers and politicians shed their suits and enjoy the experience of meeting their neighbors in their swimming costumes. The river swimming brings a kind of holiday spirit to the everyday life of the city.

River swimming is free and it is socially inclusive for a diverse group of people—young and old, different nationalities and ethnicities, locals and tourists. Even some pets join in. Since this activity is easily accessible every day after school or after work, it means there are many and frequent opportunities to connect to nature and, at the same time, make new friends and acquaintances.

Beyond the daily enjoyment, the Aare River experience informs people's broader understanding of the weather and the environment. For example, people better understand how the water temperature in the river is affected by the weather in the mountains, and take notice from year to year of the start, the end, the length, and the consistency of the swimming season. These are relevant topics of conversation as this important annual activity is so directly affected by the weather. This feeds into a deeper understanding of the weather patterns, cycles, and how it all connects to our own experiences and lives. Even for the spectator, swimming has a relevance, and the sight of river swimmers while sitting on a train or tram connects people to their place and climate.

The infrastructure that supports the river swimming is quite basic and intuitive to use. Along the riverside, there are simple concrete steps with brightly painted handrails to make getting in and out easy as well as buoys and some simple warning signs telling people when they should get out.

02.

03.

01. Jumping in from a footbridge.
02./03. Simple concrete steps and brightly painted handrails help swimmers in and out of the river.
04. Swimmers walking along the riverside.

04.

> *"There is no such thing as bad weather, only the wrong clothes."*
>
> Scandinavian saying

01. **Tokyo, Japan.** Children being children: growing up curious and responding to what's around. We cannot force anyone to do anything, but we can at least create the opportunities for encounters with nature.

02. **Berne, Switzerland.** Chess is not just a game for two. This outdoor activity attracts a small but faithful crowd and gives them a legitimate excuse to linger longer in the outdoors.

Living with the weather is about recognizing how the design of the built environment can influence our behavior, making it easy to move between inside and out, and making it comfortable to spend more time outdoors. At the same time, by taking small steps, we can move toward living more in harmony with the forces of nature in a time of climate change. Being outside means having sensory experiences, actually feeling the weather on your skin. In order to get people who live their lives indoors to develop better relationships with the outdoors, to learn to live with the weather or become better neighbors with nature, we must offer options and opportunities, frequent invitations and occasional nudges, to move closer to nature, one step at a time.

Many newly built environments such as homes, institutions, and workplaces seem to be oriented to staying indoors, and any mobility around them is based on driving. The internet age has spurred debate and research on the value of being outside and in contact with nature–especially related to the upbringing of children in an age of iPads.[33] Spending time outdoors creates opportunities for socialization, for shared experiences of natural phenomena, which in turn can help build a common understanding and consensus of what's happening with our climate.

Every city comes with its own set of climate challenges. But weather does not only have to be something that we endure. It is also possible to design outside conditions through designs to create better, simple details—such as the shape and massing of buildings and the spaces in between—that have the potential to create more comfortable microclimates. By letting the sun in, and sometimes keeping it out, by sheltering from the wind and rain, we have the potential to make our own weather, or at least to extend the time we can spend outdoors. Low-tech, low-cost interventions such as shutters and stairs, balconies and arcades can bring people out of their normal, indoor comfort zones into a closer, more satisfying relationship with the natural and social environments outside.

There is a well-known saying in Scandinavia: "There is no such thing as bad weather, only the wrong clothes."

01.

02.

Soft is Hard
to Break

01.

03.

02.

05.

04.

06.

07.

What makes human settlements last? How could Rome survive the fall of the Empire and, more than a thousand years later, be the capital of modern Italy? Dresden and Hiroshima were bombed to the ground, yet were reborn, from only dust and memories. Meanwhile, why do many new, planned cities fail to thrive? Will Brasilia ever become a Rio or will Canberra ever become a Sydney?

At the same time, there are favelas that demonstrate resilience and have much more life than heavily subsidized, planned housing projects. Arguably, some informal settlements, without architects or designers or subsidies, built on the least valuable land, have created surprisingly sustainable, inclusive, and close-knit communities, responsive to the evolving needs of their residents.

01. Copenhagen, Denmark.
With no fences or walls, this schoolyard is completely open to the public square.

02. Paris, France.
Used-book stalls inhabit the heavy protection walls along the Seine, creating employment, culture, and entertainment.

03. Barcelona, Spain.
Public information campaign promoting better behavior in public places.

04. New York City, USA.
The large, shared table in a café enables spontaneous social interaction.

05. Paris, France.
On a permeable gravel surface and under a canopy of trees, movable chairs allow limitless permutations for sitting.

06. Copenhagen, Denmark.
Hybrid travel—taking a messenger bike on the suburban train.

07. Tokyo, Japan.
Grandparents and grandchildren taking advantage of a pedestrianized street.

To make a better habitat for ourselves, we need to deal with challenges around us; and to deal with those challenges, we need to embrace them. We need to be better connected to world around us. Building walls doesn't solve the challenge of what is on the other side. In many ways, it only accentuates the problem. Instead, we need to build relationships. As we face climate change, segregation, congestion, and rapid urbanization, we need to build better relationships with the planet, with people, and with place. Building stand-alone, air-conditioned buildings up in the sky or in gated communities, or building more roads and having autonomous cars won't connect us to the global challenges or to each other, so that we can ultimately deal with them together.

The town or city is a system of relationships, a place where multiple, overlapping systems of different relationships are co-located—public and private, common and individual, formal and informal. Like the layers of nature in the forest, the multiple and interconnected relationships connect different phenomena to each other and increase the resilience of the whole.

We know from life that a strong relationship is not a rigid one. Sensitivity and responsiveness are vital components of a good relationship. Being

01.

02.

03.

04.

05.

06.

07.

08.

in control doesn't mean never changing your position. In fact, quite the opposite is true. Being in control means being able to respond appropriately at a particular moment and in a particular situation, and that response is not always going to be the same. There is give and take; there is time for opening up and time for shutting up. Soft relationships, because of their sensitivity and responsiveness, can do much more and last longer than hard ones. In this way, we might say that soft is hard to break.

Knowing that life is constantly changing, we need a physical framework that adapts and changes with us—something living, something organic, something soft.

The soft city is not just built form. Every town or city is a complex combination of hardware and software. Hardware is the physical form, the structure, the streets and buildings, everything that is designed and built. The software is made up of all the invisible structures of legislation and finance, planning and education, democracy and customs and culture, behavior and trust. This book has been mostly about the hardware of how towns and cities are built, but the software deserve just as much attention.

You can see glimpses of the soft city everywhere; low-cost, low-tech, larger and smaller phenomena, explicit or subtle tolerances and tendencies, all of which somehow, in the short term, make your everyday life more enjoyable. In the longer term, the soft city can help tackle some of the great challenges facing human beings on this planet. What they have in common is accommodating the density and diversity of everyday life, bringing the opportunity to experience a better life closer.

While the connections of people to nature and people to place are important, I believe the connection of people to other people is the most important. Only when people come together can they truly understand what they have in common, and then together explore how much is actually possible.

Winston Churchill famously said "We shape our buildings, and afterwards, our buildings shape us." From the work of Jan Gehl, Jane Jacobs, and others, we know that the physical form of environment influences our behavior. But before we decide what to build, we need to decide how we want to live our lives and what sort of world we want to live in.

And, as Jan Gehl says, "First life, then spaces, and buildings last."

01. **Lucerne, Switzerland.**
A small balcony to the courtyard connects to sunshine, tree tops and the other neighbors on their balconies.

02. **Malmö, Sweden.**
Bus stop sign with extra-large numbers counting down till departure time lets you know if you have to run to for your bus.

03. **New York, USA.**
Edible landscaping on the street.

04. **Malmö, Sweden.**
A wheeling ramp makes the underground railway station accessible for cyclists.

05. **Mexico City, Mexico.**
A "hole in the wall" window turns the sidewalk into a shop.

06. **Lucerne, Switzerland.**
Universal access, commercial activity, public space and public life—all at the same time.

07. **Kyoto, Japan.**
Giant stepping stones connect the population with the large water surface of the river.

08. **Copenhagen, Denmark.**
Even the youngest children in daycare in Denmark make frequent excursions outdoors.

Nine Criteria

for Livable Urban Density

There has been much research and writing about the potential to deliver the same density of buildings in quite different ways. All of this work shows that buildings of lower and medium rise consistently perform surprisingly well, demonstrating that you don't need higher rise to get higher density. However, few are willing to question or judge the social or environmental consequences of the different built forms.

Measurements like FAR (Floor Area Ratio) and other such formulae are not necessarily useful indicators of success since they only measure size or quantity. The performance of higher-density urban form needs to be measured in a more complex and complete way. Qualitative criteria are needed. We need to ask how the built form supports everyday life. The success of urban form must be measured in its delivery of a higher quality of life for the people who live with it and its resilience and adaptability to constant changes in society, environment, and economy.

A key focus should be on the relationships with the surroundings that a certain built form makes possible. How well does a built form connect people to the physical resources of the city, accessing the useful facilities and amenities, the things and the places? How well does a built form connect people with the forces of nature, living more in tune with the weather? How well does the built form connect people to other people, for convivial encounters and social opportunity?

Nine Criteria

When considering the potential livability and sustainability of a dense built environment, I have come up with nine criteria to assess quality.

A livable, resilient, high-density area should have: a diversity of built form and of outdoor spaces, flexibility, a human scale, walkability, a sense of control and identity, a pleasant microclimate, a smaller carbon footprint, and greater biodiversity.

Nine Criteria for Livable Urban Density

1. Diversity of Built Form

2. Diversity of Outdoor Spaces

3. Flexibility

4. Human Scale

5. Walkability

6. Sense of Control and Identity

7. A Pleasant Microclimate

8. Smaller Carbon Footprint

9. Greater Biodiversity

1. Diversity of Built Form

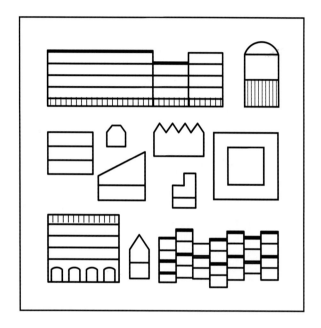

The urban form should accommodate different sizes of buildings, with only a few large and extra-large components, to leave room for greater diversity of building types and activities. There should be more extra-small, small, and medium components. There should be different typologies including small houses, apartment buildings, office buildings, larger industrial sheds, production spaces, and specialized buildings such as sport halls and houses of worship.

Ideally, different dimensions will be accommodated in close proximity, such as small houses and large houses. The buildings could also be subdivided in different ways to vary the density. For example, a large apartment building may contain many smaller apartments, and a small apartment building may house only a few larger apartments. An office building could have large, single-space floorplates or many small rooms. The urban form should be able to comfortably accommodate social housing alongside private housing, public institutions alongside commercial ventures, and corporations alongside cooperatives. Small but significant components such as "granny flats" and home offices should also be accommodated.

Having different activities coexisting is both useful and more sustainable. Dwelling, working, learning, and recreating in close proximity allows us to live more locally. To accommodate the broadest range of different, useful activities in a neighborhood, we need to accommodate the broadest range of building types. Since usefulness in everyday life comes from the proximity of different activities to each other, we need an urban form that accommodates different volumes and shapes of building. The different types should fit together in a connected whole, where one building and its activities does not overbear its neighbors.

The different buildings must be respectful and not overlook or overshadow one another, respecting the overall pattern of fronts, backs, and sides, as well as access to public or common infrastructure. The greater the diversity of space within a building, the greater the likelihood of accommodating a diversity of neighbors. The independent components should function as a greater whole.

For a sustainable and resilient society, we need to accommodate different kinds of people, and balance public- and private-sector activity. We need an urban form that accommodates different kinds of tenure and management. Subdivision of land into smaller properties allows for a broader range of ownership and control.

Each individual building has the potential to create spatial difference within itself. In particular, the built form should acknowledge that some parts of the building are connected to the ground plane, which gives certain affordances such as easier access. Other parts of the building are connected to the sky, and this affords more light. And then there is the part of the building in the middle, between these two, that will be different again. Some buildings, like big single-story sheds, might have all three aspects at once. There might also be basements, which are conveniently close to the ground plane for access but obviously have less natural light.

The diversity of buildings and their combination should create visual variation. The juxtaposition of different appearances can contribute a sense of place, making for more interesting sensory experiences and a greater feeling of identity, both for individuals and for a community. These visual differences make a street or neighborhood more distinct and recognizable, which aids orientation and makes walking more enjoyable.

Densely built, urban form should accommodate a broad range of building types (different typologies, shapes, dimensions, and spatial conditions) in close proximity to each other. Buildings should be physically respectful of each other while remaining organizationally independent.

What to look for

- Different kinds of buildings

- Different dimensions

- Different typologies

- Smaller plots

- Smaller subdivisions

- Smaller and more-diverse ownership

- Balance of building component parts: ground floor, middle, and top

- Visual variation

2. Diversity of Outdoor Spaces

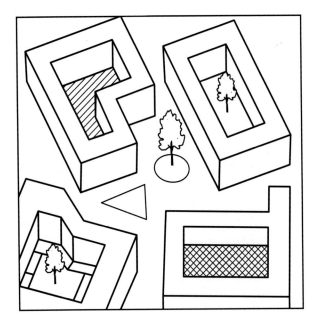

It should be easy and enjoyable to spend more time outdoors. Spending time outdoors can connect people to their surroundings and to each other. It's about having more kinds of outdoor space to accommodate more kinds of outdoor life.

The outdoor spaces of a town or city are important because they provide vital, extra, useful living space in the otherwise more compact and confined urban environment. The greater the diversity of the spaces, the greater the potential for activities to take place as well as the greater diversity of such activities. Using outdoor spaces should be part of everyday life, which means putting a higher value on the space right outside your front door. It's not just the pleasure of gardening or trips to the park, but all of the everyday things that have to be done; waiting for the bus or putting out the garbage should be opportunities for pleasurable encounters.

Spending time outdoors means fresh air, physical activity, and meeting people, all of which can contribute to better physical and mental health.

The outdoor spaces of the city should make up a system of diverse public and private places, joined up or juxtaposed. The combination and interconnection of different types of space makes for a complex system, the nuances of which allow more activity to happen.

Public spaces like streets, squares, and parks offer something different than private spaces like gardens and courtyards. If both types can exist in close proximity to each other and complement one another, greater choice and opportunity can be delivered to more people in everyday life. As with other aspects of the city, the whole is greater than the sum of the parts.

The urban form needs to accommodate not only both public and private outdoor spaces, but also different kinds of public spaces and different kinds of private spaces in close proximity. There should be different dimensions—small spaces and large, intimate and grand—along with different access arrangements and levels of privacy, from the highly visible to the completely hidden.

Between public and private, there are subcategories such as "semi-public" and "semi-private," common and shared, the exact definitions of which could be discussed at length. What is important is that there should be a range of these different types of spaces.

There should also be robust, flexible, multipurpose spaces with flexibility to allow different things to happen at different times. There should also be spaces dedicated to specific activities such as sports, games, and performances.

There are also different kinds of hybrid "inside-outside" spaces that connect the buildings to the outdoors. These might include colonnades, arcades, decks, balconies, porches, verandas, loggias, terraces, and roof gardens.

Finally, streets are also public spaces. There are different kinds of streets, from boulevards, avenues, and main streets to side streets, back streets, mews, alleys, and laneways, all of which can support outdoor life in different ways. Streets that have been planned as traffic conduits may, in fact, be important places for people, in which standing, staying, and sitting are as important as moving through. In the same way, other outdoor spaces might be places of movement. For example, a city park or square might be part of someone's route to work or a shared courtyard garden might be a shortcut for someone else.

Dense, urban form should accommodate different kinds of outdoor spaces, in close proximity to each other, in response to the wide spectrum of needs for public and private life.

What to look for

- Different kinds of public outdoor spaces

- Different kinds of private outdoor spaces

- Different kinds of shared/common outdoor spaces

- Different typologies of space that respond to different needs and activities, from the very general to the most specific

- Hybrid spaces that connect inside and out

- Streets as public spaces

- Public spaces as places for mobility

3. Flexibility

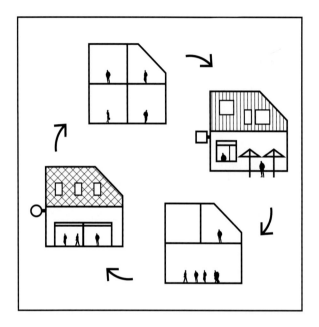

Life is in constant change, and the town, city, or neighborhood is never finished. If a place is to be truly resilient, its urban form must be responsive to and capable of change. It must adapt to changing demographics and economic cycles, densification, new activities and functions, new people, and established residents with new and changing needs. A neighborhood has to be able to respond to change in the shorter, medium, and longer term.

Shorter-term changes might depend on the day (weekday or weekend), the time of day, the season, or the weather. A flexible space is multipurpose to accommodate these changing needs—a school playground that becomes a public park on the weekend, a market square that can also be used as a carpark, a church hall that is used by the scouts during the week, or a hotel or office lobby that becomes a pop-up store.

Perhaps the most modest and fleeting potential for change is when the ground floor has the potential to spill out. This can be very valuable for spaces such as cafés or restaurants with tables and chairs spilling over onto the sidewalk or into the courtyard, a shop displaying goods outside, or residents invading the edge zone around the door with potted plants, outdoor furniture, and parked cycles.

Courtyards are particularly flexible spaces. There is something about the simple containment of enclosed spaces that makes accommodating change easier. Because they are visually hidden and acoustically muffled, enclosed spaces like courtyards change easily since they don't disturb the surroundings.

In the medium term, changes might mean a building changing use, a renovation, or a small extension, responding to the need for growth or for greater personalization. A small, local increase in density may allow a growing family or an expanding business to stay in the same location.

Having direct access from the public realm to a space increases the potential for a change of use. Neutral access can be walking straight in from the street, or having an independent, private staircase only serving the premises in question, or in the case of a building inside a courtyard, access through a passageway would also work. Ideally, the new uses and users will not directly disturb existing uses and users (see also criterion 5 on walkability). Ground floor spaces are the most likely to change use as they have direct access to and from the public realm. Importantly, with this direct access, the ground floor can change use without disturbing rest of the building. In very general terms, the larger the proportion of a ground floor with direct access, the more flexible the building is and the greater potential to change uses. If the ground-floor space is subdivided with independent units, it will have greater flexibility. The more independent spaces there are, the greater the opportunity for spontaneous change.

Ancillary buildings and spaces are particularly useful in accommodating change, including densification, as there is no controversy of introducing new volumes. It's only a question of reclassifying the existing buildings or spaces, perhaps with minor physical changes and upgrading. Basements, attics, and outbuildings are all useful spaces for accommodating densification, from the inside. Outbuildings have the advantage of having direct, walk-straight-in ground-floor access, albeit most likely from a courtyard space rather than the street. Attics, in particular, are interesting as the roof space offers the potential for different type spaces, in terms of light and layout, to be added. The basement is not as attractive as the attic floor since it cannot accommodate as many uses. However, proximity to the ground floor and the street means commercial uses are possible. The more attic, the more basement, and the more outbuildings can mean greater potential for change of use.

A clear structure with backs and fronts can be more tolerant to change over time as there is perceived room for growth. In an already built-up area, extensions to the rear are more readily accepted, as the visual impact of the changes are not visible to many.

In the longer term, flexibility should allow for the removal and replacement of larger components such as entire buildings without disturbing the built form as a whole. Therefore, urban form that is made up of multiple, independent constructions or *fractals*, which allow local demolishing and replacement, can accommodate larger, more-significant changes.

Dense and diverse urban form, with both buildings and spaces, should be flexible and responsive to change (including densification), at all scales, in the short, medium, and long term.

What to look for

- Multipurpose spaces, indoors and outdoors

- A greater proportion of built volume is ground floor

- Independent access to different parts of a building (especially direct access from the public realm)

- Ancillary spaces such as outbuildings, basements, and attics

- Backs with room for growth

- Enclosure spaces that can contain activities

- Room on the edge of buildings for temporary overflow

- Independent fractals

4. Human Scale

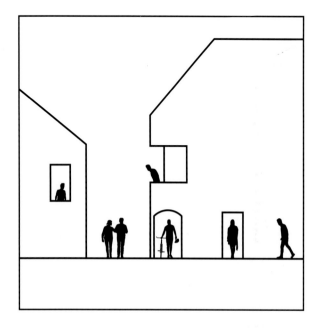

If we recognize the needs of people in urban spaces, taking care of the environment with protection, comfort, and pleasure in mind, we can make neighborhoods that people will want to go to, go through, and spend time in.

Human scale in general terms means dimensions rooted in the human senses and behavior, resulting in smaller built components and lower heights. In particular, it means designing with attention to the experience at eye level, including appealing to sensory stimuli, and using dimensions that relate to the human body.

Smaller spaces bring people closer to each other and closer to things. Being in close proximity to the sensory system, close enough to see small details, close enough to distinguish small sounds, close enough to smell, and close enough to touch, intensifies encounters and experiences. The smaller dimensions can also

deliver better microclimates in the in-between spaces, meaning a more pleasant bodily experience. Smaller spaces also give a greater sense of security as people have a comfortable overview of a place.

Walk-up-height buildings help maintain a connection between the ground plane and the upper floors. This is the distance at which your eyes can focus and gain useful information, your voice can carry, and your hearing can distinguish different sounds. Buildings up to five stories usually meet these criteria.

Smaller spaces can be secure and comfortable places in which to spend time and meet people. There is a kind of psychological coziness that comes with certain smaller spaces, something comforting and calming that promotes intimacy and sociability.

Smallness can humanize a larger-scale environment, as if people are somehow programmed to focus on the smaller things because we know that they are most likely to be the most rewarding. Therefore, the presence of smaller built elements among larger ones is important.

An urban environment should appeal to all the senses. It is not just about what you see, although visual stimulation is important. The more opportunities to observe living phenomena the better—seeing other people doing activities, viewing the big sky, shadows and light, flowers and trees, and birds and animals. Seeing a diversity of color and materials, as well as a variety of patterns and decoration, is also important.

The human being is designed to walk and has the greatest capacity to interpret, engage with, and respond to the surrounding environment at eye-level. The face is where the human senses are concentrated and also where we communicate and express the most emotion. What happens at eye level as we enter a space on foot, as we meet our surroundings, is the most significant. Therefore, the urban form has to perform best at the level of the ground floor.

What happens in the first three vertical meters (ten feet) of experience connects us to the place. It connects us to the buildings with the windows and doors, the materials, textures and colors, but also to the people, where they walk, stand, and sit. Since the eye-level experience is a continuous one as we move through space, it is important that the scene is constantly changing, and we are continually presented with new stimuli.

Human beings are highly sensitive to unpleasant physical and climatic phenomena. When there is an interruption or disconnect between one place and another because of a bad experience, patterns of behavior are lost, and people are much less likely walk or spend time in that place. The quality of human-scale elements such as smaller dimensions, sensory experiences, and care at eye-level, should be consistent through a neighborhood and not just exist in isolated spots.

Urban form should deliver density at a human scale, meaning at dimensions and with details that can offer comfort and well-being to people living in and around the buildings and the spaces in between.

What to look for

- Smaller dimensions

- Smaller spaces

- No higher than six stories—ideally four or five

- Multi-sensory experiences

- Particular care for the eye-level experience

- Consistent quality at eye level

5. Walkability

Walkability refers to the smallest, but perhaps most important, movements that people make every day. Designing for walkability is about connecting people to the life of their neighborhood, seeing what is available, and having options to access it. The goal is quick-and-easy access, convenience, spontaneous participation, and being able to get from one situation to another quickly and easily.

Within buildings, it is about the seemingly simple things such as frequency, position, and function of windows, doors, halls, passages, and staircases, which create options for complex movement. It is about making a walkable neighborhood that is protected, comfortable, and pleasant, with easy movement from building to building, from building to block, from block to block, and from neighborhood to surroundings. Walkability is also about relationships—getting to know people and places and experiencing the forces of nature on the way.

The ground floor is extremely valuable because it is the most accessible. It allows everyone to enter or exit directly, which is the easiest application of universal access. This inside-outside mobility is useful for the busiest uses such as shops, workplaces, institutions, and even homes.

Every building with a shared staircase should have access to the front and to the back, to give choices. Every individual house should have a front and a back door. The pend, or passageway, creates a dynamic connection between the public and the private of the city.

The value of the walk-up is being able to access as much of a building as possible without being dependent on an elevator, as well as retaining a sensory connection to what is happening at ground level. A good test question for any built environment is what proportion can be reached without requiring the use of an elevator.

A small but significant detail is the location of common staircases. Ideally, they will be on the outside wall of buildings and have windows, giving natural light and ventilation, as well as a constant connection with the outside. Dog-leg stairs, which shift direction every half floor, break both physical and visual tedium, as you are given a little rest and are spared the view of the long flight of stairs.

Windows are important for light and to make people aware of the life outside, connecting people to climate. The shape of the window can affect the relationship with the outside. Not only does a vertical window opening take up less useable space on the inside, it lets light penetrate more deeply into a room, affords views of the sky, the surrounding buildings and trees, and life down on the ground.

While windows are valuable, doors are the real connectors, as they make physical access possible. There is a vital connection that comes from street-watching, being able to get straight outside, and to participating in what is happening on the street. More-frequent doors mean more easy and spontaneous movement from one kind of space to another, between inside and outside, and from private to public realms. Front doors and back doors are equally valuable. Bonus openings like French windows and patio doors, or extra, eccentric features like private outdoor staircases, add to the probability of more frequent inside-outside movement. My own simple rule for buildings is that if you can see the window of the apartment, you should be able to see an entrance door of some kind.

The urban form should allow for a small but useful space right outside dwellings and workplaces, so that you can literally step outside. Balconies, loggias, roof terraces, porches, verandas, front stoops, back steps, small front and back garden zones all fall into this category.

The built form should allow for easy accessibility and connectedness. In the simplest terms, accessibility is about being able to move quickly with the least amount of effort, in, out, and through buildings and between as many different spaces and places as possible. It also means walkability at a neighborhood scale, with walking as the most comfortable and convenient option for short distances.

What to look for:

- Walk-in buildings

- Walk-through buildings

- Walk-up buildings

- A higher proportion of ground floor

- Visual connection and physical access between inside and outside

- Direct access to useful outside spaces

- Walkability at the neighborhood scale

6. A Sense of Control and Identity

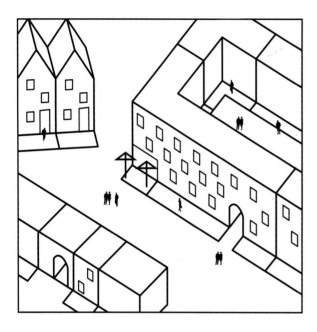

The built form should be made up of identifiable, distinct places, physically defined, that belong to or are controlled by an individual or group.

It could be as small as a recessed step in front of a doorway where the resident can put a potted plant. It could be a small, private garden in front of a house or a ground-floor apartment where the resident can have some furniture and plant some shrubs. It could be a common staircase shared by eight families, where everyone knows each other well enough to be able ask for help in a minor emergency. It could be a back courtyard shared by a few buildings where play equipment is shared and common activities can take place. It could also be a local street with a sense of identity or a public square that is accessible to all.

The hierarchy of territories starts in the home, which might have some subtle layering, with common zones including living rooms and kitchens, and more-private ones including bedrooms and bathrooms.

The next layer is the group of apartments sharing an address and the people living around a common staircase, making a small, exclusive group with the very specific shared interest of living in the same place, balancing acquaintance, respect, tolerance, and strictness.

The next layer is a shared, common outdoor space, such as a garden or courtyard. This is a larger and more-diverse group than the staircase neighbors, made up of people who have some common interest in cleanliness, safety, security, and quietness at night. Then, there is the identity of belonging to a group of people who live and work along a certain street or around a certain public space.

The next level is the neighborhood. This is the real test of success. If there is no sense of identity there, it may be necessary to jump to the next layer of the town or city.

The structure of the built environment can make defined spaces, which can be recognizable places. For example, on a larger scale, a block of joined-up buildings may have a clear outside and inside, with fronts and backs, and a clear differentiation between public and private. This creates distinct courtyards and gardens on the inside and public spaces, streets, and squares on the outside that are clearly identifiable places. At the small scale, devices such as small walls or hedges, gates, and gateways might be enough to define a territory.

Social phenomena like public and private can translate very easily into the spatial phenomena of fronts and backs. The front, the more exposed side, has a certain formality. It is generally tidier, more strictly controlled, and there is an understanding and acceptance of rules and a certain kind of behavior. The back, because it is more hidden, is generally much more informal and relaxed. There is greater freedom and acceptance of individual, personal expression. A shop window display and a neat flower garden might be on the front while the garbage cans, cycle storage, and hanging laundry are hidden at the back.

Edge zones, particularly those outside homes, are important for expressing identity. For example, a small, private garden or deck allows the resident to use the space as they want—whether for planting, storage, decoration, or as a social space. Every household has different specific needs. A private edge zone allows and even celebrates these differences.

Corners are important as significant and recognizable nodes in the spatial system of the neighborhood. The corner is a place where two or more paths meet, a significant intersection in the mobility network, where you can change direction. It seems universal that corners are favored places to meet, valuable locations for successful commercial activity (like cafés and popular local shops), and opportunities for architectural expression in buildings, thanks to the multiple views they afford. The combination of all of these—network location, significant business activity, and memorable architecture—make corners potentially more useful places, and help orientation in a neighborhood.

Finally, it is important that the public spaces feel genuinely public and people feel welcome to come and spend time there.

The built form should offer people, as individuals and in smaller and larger groups, better control over the spaces around them. The spaces should foster a sense of identity as well as aid orientation and navigation.

What to look for:

- A hierarchy of identifiable territories
- Clarity between public and private
- Fronts and backs
- Enclosure and spatial clarity
- Smaller units and subdivisions
- Common/shared spatial focus
- Useful edge zones
- Significant corners

7. A Pleasant Microclimate

The physical comfort from good microclimate is particularly important for public life, encouraging walking, cycling, and spending time outdoors. It is also important for public transport use, as this also entails walking and spending time outside waiting. As already mentioned in criterion 2 addressing living outdoors, spending time in the spaces between buildings can compensate for the more confined living conditions typical of urban life.

Working with built form and microclimate is about softening the weather, not denying or changing it. It is a process of filtering out the extremes. Similar to the notion of "dressing for the weather," it is about helping people to be more at one with their climate by bringing them closer to it. It also means less reliance on mechanical heating and cooling.

In order to make a livelier neighborhood and to encourage more sustainable behavior, and in particular active mobility, the pleasant microclimate should start right outside of your front door. This is the place where you start your walk, the route that takes you to the bus stop (or wherever you are going), and even the place where you wait. It is important not just to create exceptional pockets of pleasant climate, but to create a pleasant climate throughout the urban form. Jan Gehl often observes that this quality was built into most older city districts.

An urban form that is consistent with lower building heights almost always creates a better microclimate because there are no tall structures to cause turbulence. Taller buildings frequently catch stronger and colder winds, and divert them down toward the ground, making the in-between spaces unpleasant, colder, and windswept. Additionally, tall buildings cast longer shadows, keeping places in the dark and cold.

Buildings with aerodynamic roof shapes such as pitched, hipped, rounded, or mansard can help to divert the stronger winds away from the ground plane and let the sun penetrate down into the in-between spaces.

When sunny edges and wind protection are combined, such as in courtyards, sun traps are created, which are particularly useful places for outdoor life when the weather is colder. Interestingly, enclosed spaces like courtyards can also be useful in hotter climates, providing shade as well as thermal storage for the colder nights. Semi-enclosed spaces such as recessed balconies can have a longer useful season.

Small details such as openings can be significant for microclimatic experience. French windows and Dutch barn/stable doors can effectively turn a whole room into a balcony, and connect people indoors to the fresh air and life outside.

Rain shouldn't stop the daily movements of neighborhood life. Smaller and larger features in the built form can allow movement and spending time outdoors to continue even when it is wet. This type of protective building architecture includes smaller interventions like overhangs, canopies, awnings, and generous projecting eaves along the edge of a building, as well as larger-scale options such as colonnades, arcades, and covered walkways.

Creating a pleasant microclimate with a built form allows people to spend more time outdoors.

What to look for:

- Consistent microclimatic conditions throughout a space

- Protection from strong winds and avoidance of turbulence

- Solar penetration and avoidance of shadows

- Aerodynamic roof shape

- Protected or enclosed outdoor spaces

- Useful openings

- Rain protection at edges

8. Smaller Carbon Footprint

The built form should have a minimum negative effect on the environment. The layout, size, and shape of buildings can translate into lower energy use, less pollution as well as saving natural resources and materials (and money).

There are immediate benefits from lower building heights and enclosed spaces, which create better local microclimates. Reduced exposure to strong wind and sun can mean less maintenance, as well as reducing the need for artificial heating and cooling in the whole area. Having more joined-up buildings means that there are not as many exposed sides, reducing construction costs, and, over time, reducing heating and cooling costs in the individual buildings.

There is no substitute for natural light. There are considerable energy savings and benefits to health and well-being when indoor spaces have natural light.

Ideally, all rooms and communication spaces will be naturally lit. Smaller building dimensions allow for more spaces to be lit from more than one side, greatly improving the indoor light experience over the course of the day. It is important to consider the quality of light throughout the day and not just the quantity of light at a specific hour, as many building codes and standards do. With narrower buildings, there is a greater possibility of having natural light everywhere indoors. With lower buildings, it is more possible to use skylights to greater effect.

With thinner and lower buildings, natural ventilation is possible up to a certain height—generally, up to eight stories using conventional technology and building systems. And with natural light, there are considerable energy savings and benefits to health and well-being. Countless books have been written about sick-building syndrome and the societal costs of people suffering from spending time in unhealthy buildings because of artificial lighting and ventilation.

In an urban form with greater ground coverage, there is also more roof, and potential for solar harvesting and greening to reduce heat-island effect. The sunny rooftops also make ideal positions for greenhouses for local food production.

An urban form based on lower and smaller buildings can be built with simple (lighter) construction. The use of a healthy and renewable material such as wood is possible using conventional and common building practices. This saves on embedded energy as well as pollution involved in the production of materials like concrete and steel. The lower and smaller scale also works well for prefabrication, which, thanks to precision building, has generally far better environmental performance than standard construction methods.

Lighter buildings have lighter, shallower foundations, which mean less damage to subsoils and the water table, and savings on embedded energy.

Lower buildings mean there is less reliance on elevators. Less elevator use means less energy in production and building operation.

However, the real environmental benefit is the energy savings that come from everyday behavior with a more walkable neighborhood—with people being able to access what they need every day, without relying on an automobile.

The built form should use fewer resources in construction and operation while promoting behaviors and lifestyles with a smaller carbon foot print, such as walking and cycling.

What to look for:

- Fewer exposed facades (thanks to joined-up buildings)

- Smaller dimenions to allow natural light and ventilation

- Simpler construction and foundation systems

- Less reliance on complex technology and heavy engineering

- Layout promoting active mobility (especially walking)

9. Greater Biodiversity

The built form should allow green spaces and natural life to thrive. There are many benefits of biodiversity, both to people and to the planet. This is mainly about vegetation, but considering a more holistic biodiversity. This also affects insect, bird, and animal life.

There are clear benefits to health and well-being for urban dwellers with richer and more-diverse nature in otherwise built-up areas. Vegetation has an acoustic effect, absorbing and masking amidst the many hard surfaces of walls and paving in the urban context (and hence reducing stress). It also has the ability to help mitigate pollution, cleansing the air by absorbing dangerous nanoparticles, which is important considering the frequency of respiratory diseases in urban areas. Vegetation is also practical as visual screening, increasing privacy as well as reducing and mitigating wind, and protecting from strong summer sun. Vegetation can help to mitigate the heat-island effect.

A greater number of property subdivisions can lead to greater biodiversity because of potentially different kinds of control, standards, and approaches to gardening and wildness. Each property can have characteristics to potentially make a unique micro-ecosystem. But when put together, all of these individual plots make for even greater biodiversity. There is a local climax of biodiversity at the threshold where two different systems meet, for example along the hedges, fences, and garden walls between subdivisions. In this way, both the different conditions of each subdivision as well as the climax along their edges makes for biodiversity. The whole is greater than the sum of its parts.

Balancing solar access and wind protection, enclosure or partial enclosure helps create a favorable microclimate (see also criterion 7) for growing conditions and reduces disturbance from human footfall. Physically protected spaces like courtyards and walled gardens allow flora and fauna to flourish. They are also places where people can enjoy nature less disturbed. For example, the acoustic effect of vegetation and wildlife noise (trees rustling and birds singing) is much stronger in a more protected space.

Consistently lower building heights create a better microclimate for green roofs (from roof gardens with potted plants to sedum and planted roof surfaces) and green walls (from simple creeper plants to complex planting systems). The whole range of small, plantable spaces from window boxes to balconies work better in the milder microclimate created by lower building heights.

The built form should generate spaces to accommodate soft landscaping as well as local water management and filtration of rainwater. There should be numerous and frequent places with deeper soil to allow natural drainage. Too often, underground structures such as carparks eliminate the possibility of natural drainage or tree planting over large areas. With a smaller scale of buildings and hard surfaces, the quantity of stormwater run-off is reduced and is therefore more manageable.

The closer nature is to your everyday life, the more relevant it becomes. As mentioned in criterion 6, the thoughtful arrangement of the buildings in relation to their surroundings and in-between outdoor spaces can increase a sense of control, responsibility, and community.

The more easily accessible the outdoor spaces are, the greater the likelihood of frequent and regular use, and, in turn, a sense of care that invites tending and nurturing behaviors, perhaps resulting in shared community-garden work and even community harvesting. Therefore, a scale and division of land that makes courtyards, gardens, and allotments possible, with clearly defined private and shared spaces, allows for responsibility and connection to the natural world.

Urban form should accommodate natural life. The layout, size, and shape of the buildings and use of spaces should accommodate natural life and make greater biodiversity possible.

Things to look for:

- Multiplicity of smaller, individual outdoor green spaces

- Many protected spaces and edges

- Smaller dimensions of buildings to allow green walls and roofs to thrive

- Smaller scale for water management with slower water filtration

- Soft landscaping where possible

Notes

Notes

Introduction

1   Inger Christensen, *It*, trans. Susanna Nied (New York: New Directions 2006), originally published in Danish in 1969.

2   Jan Gehl, *Life between Buildings*, trans. Jo Koch (Washington D.C.: Island Press 2011, originally published in Danish in 1971.)

3   Jan Gehl, *Life between Buildings*, trans. Jo Koch (Washington D.C.: Island Press 2011, originally published in Danish in 1971.) Ingrid Gehl, Bomiljø, (Copenhagen: SBI Rapport 71, 1971).

4   See *Monocle*'s Quality of Life Survey in which Copenhagen was nominated Most Livable City three times (2008, 2013, 2014). It was number one in *Metropolis*'s rankings in 2016; and in the *Economist*, it came in at number nine on the city livability ranking from 2005-2018.

5   Jaime Lerner, *Planning Report*, October 2007: https://www.planning report.com/2007/11/01/jaime-lerner -cities-present-solutions-not-prob lems-quality-life-climate-change (accessed 14 April 2019).

Building Blocks

6   City of Copenhagen, Green Court-yards program, established in 1992.

7   Jane Jacobs, *The Death and Life of Great American Cities* (New York: Random House 1961).

8   Karsten Pålsson, *Public Spaces and Urbanity: How to Design Humane Cities.* Construction and Design Manual (Berlin: DOM Publishers 2017), 164.

9   G. J. Coates, "The Sustainable Urban District of Vauban in Freiburg, Germany," *Int. J. of Design & Nature and Ecodynamics.* Vol. 8, No. 4 (2013), 265–286.

10   Active ground floors allow for more people spending time. A study carried out with similar street layouts, but different ground floors—active (with door openings, niches, etc) versus inactive (without windows, door openings, etc)—demonstrated that seven times more people stop at the active ground floors compared to the inactive. Gehl, Jan. Kaefer, Lotte Johansen, Reigstad, Solvejg. "Close encounters with buildings" in *Urban Design International (2006) 11, 29-47.*

Time of Your Life

11   John Lennon, Beautiful Boy (1980).

Getting About and Getting On

12   Jane Jacobs, *The Death and Life of Great American Cities* (New York: Random House 1961), 36-37.

13   ITDP, Pedestrians First. *Tools for a Walkable City* (ITDP, 2018).

14   See Jan Gehl. *Cities for People* (Washington D.C.: Island Press 2010).

15   Jan Gehl. *Cities for People* (Washington D.C.: Island Press 2010), 131-32.

16   Streets should make up for 30% of the area of a city according to UN Habitat: UN Habitat, *Streets as Public Spaces and Drivers of Urban Prosperity* (UN Habitat, Nairobi: 2013).

17   City of Perth: *Two Way Streets* (City of Perth 2014); more on the disadvantage of one way streets in Vikash V. Gaya, "Two-Way Street Networks: More Efficient than Previously Thought?" in *Access*, 41, Fall 2012.

18   City of Perth: *Two Way Streets* (City of Perth 2014).

19   Rob Adams et al., *Transforming Australian Cities* (City of Melbourne: 2009).

20   Rob Adams et al., *Transforming Australian Cities* (City of Melbourne: 2009).

21   Accidents have been reduced by half according to: Allan Quimby and James Castle, *A Review of Simplified Streetscape Schemes* (London: Transport for London 2006).

22   Chinese saying.

Living With the Weather

23   On the concept of outdoor life in Scandinavia called *Friluftsliv* see Maddy Savage, *Friluftsliv the nordic concept of getting outdoors* (BBC 11 December 2017).

24   City of Copenhagen, *Bicycle Account* (City of Copenhagen 2006).

25   Numbers for 1986, 1995, 2005 from Jan Gehl, *Cities for People* (Washington D.C.: Island Press 2010), 146. 2015 numbers from City of Copenhagen, Bylivsregnskab (Public life account) (City of Copenhagen 2015), 6.

26   Christopher Bergland, "Exposure to Natural Light Improves Workplace Performance," *Psychology Today*, June 2013.

27   Christopher Alexander, *A Pattern Language: Towns, Buildings, Construction* (New York: Oxford University Press 1977), pattern 159.

28   International Energy Agency, *The Future of Cooling* (International Energy Agency, May 2018).

29   Henning Larsen, Micki Aaen Petersen, *Mikroklima analyser* (Microclimate analysis), Bo01, Västra Hamnen, Malmö, Juni 2018.

30   Henning Larsen, Micki Aaen Petersen, *Mikroklima analyser* (Microclimate analysis), Bo01, Västra Hamnen, Malmö, Juni 2018.

31   City of Melbourne, *Urban Forest Strategy*: https://www.melbourne

.vic.gov.au/community/parks-open
-spaces/urban-forest/Pages/urban
-forest-strategy.aspx (accessed
05.12.2018).

32 City of Copenhagen, *Climate
    Adaptation Plan* in English, see:
    https://en.klimatilpasning.dk/media
    /568851/copenhagen_adaption_plan
    .pdf (accessed 14 April 2019).

33 See Richard Louv, *Last Child in the
    Woods* (Chapel Hill, NC: Algonquin
    Books 2008).

About Island Press

Since 1984, the nonprofit organization Island Press has been stimulating, shaping, and communicating ideas that are essential for solving environmental problems worldwide. With more than 1,000 titles in print and some 30 new releases each year, we are the nation's leading publisher on environmental issues. We identify innovative thinkers and emerging trends in the environmental field. We work with world-renowned experts and authors to develop cross-disciplinary solutions to environmental challenges.

Island Press designs and executes educational campaigns, in conjunction with our authors, to communicate their critical messages in print, in person, and online using the latest technologies, innovative programs, and the media. Our goal is to reach targeted audiences—scientists, policy makers, environmental advocates, urban planners, the media, and concerned citizens—with information that can be used to create the framework for long-term ecological health and human well-being.

Island Press gratefully acknowledges major support from The Bobolink Foundation, Caldera Foundation, The Curtis and Edith Munson Foundation, The Forrest C. and Frances H. Lattner Foundation, The JPB Foundation, The Kresge Foundation, The Summit Charitable Foundation, Inc., and many other generous organizations and individuals.

The opinions expressed in this book are those of the author(s) and do not necessarily reflect the views of our supporters.